REBELS UNITE!

BUILD A POSITIVE REBELLION

CREATE NEW EDUCATION FUTURES

John W. Moravec

Contents

Acknowledgements

Manifesto 25 and this book were never solitary projects. From the earliest drafts of the first declaration to this companion book, it grew through conversation, critique, encouragement, and generosity from friends and colleagues around the world. I am grateful to everyone who lent a voice and pressed me to think more deeply about what education could and should become.

I thank Gustavo Andrade, Chris Bagley, Constanze Beyer, Paola Boccia, Edwin De Bree, Vivian Breucker, Alexandra Castro Ferrada, María Mercedes Civarolo, Cristóbal Cobo, Antonio L. Delgado Pérez, Claudia Dikmans, Albus Duc Hoang, Kristina House, Silvia Enriquez, Tomas C. Ferber, Richard Fransham, Gustavo Garcia Lutz, Peter Gray, Christel Hartkamp, Pekka Ihanainen, Marcel Kampman, Bob Kartous, Kateřina Kolínková, Kamila Koutná, Florian Kretzschmar, Nicola Kriesel, Luis R. Lara, Diego Leal, Carlos Lizárraga Celaya, María Cristina Martínez-Bravo, Juraj Mazák, Alejandra Mendoza Garza, Farid Mokhtar Noriega, María Mercedes Moravec, Daniel Navarrete, Varlei Xavier Nogueira, Alejandro Núñez Urquijo, Hugo Pardo Kuklinski, Alejandro Pisanty, Lucas Potenza, Noemi Pulido, Luis Napoleón Quintanilla, Dinant Roode, Javier José Simon, Alison Snieckus, Max Ugaz, Paloma Valdivia Vizarreta, David Vidal, Evangelos Vlachakis, Tim Weinert, Monika Wernz, and Alex Wiedemann.

This book carries your fingerprints. It is stronger, sharper, and more hopeful because of the ideas, doubts, and courage you shared. Thank you for walking with me as we imagine and build better futures for education.

Special thanks to Martine Eyzenga, who gave the book its visual life and a home on these pages.

And thank you, the reader. The future not predetermined. *Manifesto 25* is not a script but an invitation to join a shared vision and language for building new futures. What comes next depends on how you act, question, and create in your own context. This manifesto will change as you make it your own, as you test it, reshape it, and carry it into places I could not reach alone. Reclaiming education belongs to all of us, and its story unfolds through what you choose to do.

Preface

Nothing is more political than education. Like politics, it stands at a breaking point. The old assurances that schools would open doors, guarantee mobility, and prepare people for the future are coming apart in real time. Institutions built on those promises strain under their own contradictions. Classrooms stay full. Degrees keep flowing. Ceremonies proceed as always, while the meaning beneath them grows thin. Public trust in education as a path to progress erodes month by month. We face a stark paradox. Never have so many people around the world pursued formal schooling, and never has its value felt so uncertain. Algorithms rearrange the boundary between fact and fiction. The rise of authoritarian power narrows what people can say or do. The shadow reaches into daily life, beyond abstraction.

The cracks are easy to see. The factory model of schooling, a product of industrial modernity, shaped education to meet the needs of bureaucracies and assembly lines. The industrial assembly line lives on in age-graded cohorts, bells that dictate the beginning and end of thought, and standardized curricula that treat teachers as delivery mechanisms. Students conform to institutional routines, while institutions rarely adapt to students. Sorting, compliance, and efficiency overshadow inquiry. Curriculum narrows into checklists. Young people learn to game the system for grades and credentials even when real learning is thin. Many learn to hide curiosity to survive.

The social contract that once animated this system has broken. The promise of "work hard, achieve, and secure a happy retirement" no longer matches lived realities. Graduates face precarious labor markets, rising costs, and widening inequality. Credentials function less as gateways than as costly filters. Institutions, meanwhile, extend study and debt not to support growth but to delay a reckoning with economies unable to absorb the graduates they produce. The system sustains itself by promising more than it delivers and monetizing the gap.

This is a cultural crisis as much as an economic one. The rituals of lectures, exams, and graduations can feel like theater when outcomes fail to meet expectations. Families press children to succeed out of fear rather than confidence. Even those who excel by institutional measures often describe a misalignment between what they were taught and the realities they face. Trust erodes in schools, in leadership, and in the very idea of education as a public good.

In this vacuum, authoritarian politics thrive. Power tests how far it can push before people rebel. We see it now, as I write, in Minneapolis, where federal force meets neighborhood resistance with weapons, surveillance, and intimidation. From this city to many others, the march away from freedom spreads. Schools are pulled into culture wars. Unitary executive power defines which topics are permissible. Textbooks are sanitized. Libraries face censorship campaigns. Teachers are monitored. Dissent is punished. The rhetoric of restoring discipline, returning to standards, and protecting children sounds protective, yet it suffocates because it is used as a weapon against children. Inquiry becomes disloyalty. Complexity becomes a threat. The classroom becomes a stage for political control, not a space for thought.

THE MORAL ANCHOR:
WHEN THE PEOPLE RESIST, THE HABITS LEARNED IN CLASSROOMS DECIDE WHETHER THEY ACQUIESCE OR STAND BESIDE THEIR NEIGHBORS.

Of course, I write from one place and one history, aware that other regions reached this crisis by different paths, through colonial extraction, linguistic exclusion, and uneven access to power. Yet struggles over power, and the tools used to shape learning, echo across cultures.

Existing pressures tighten, and their pace and scope outrun every familiar response. Artificial intelligence and allied technologies remake knowledge, work, and human interaction, yet schools answer by mechanizing habits that already failed. Platforms sold as innovation sort learners, monitor attention, and predict behavior with a precision no person should wield. Algorithms enforce obedience without pathways for appeal. Instruction changes little; the apparatus of control accelerates exponentially with computational power.

This failure is dangerous. Technologies, especially AI, are not built to serve education; they are built to serve markets and the interests of a few owners. They can reinforce bias, expand surveillance, and commodify student data. When institutions resist adaptation, they convert students into data sources and training material for platforms they do not control. Obsolescence and exploitation become features of the system, not consequences. The challenge is not to fit AI into schooling as it exists, but to reimagine education in light of what these technologies mean for learning, agency, and human futures.

Meanwhile, planet-wide crises demand new forms of learning to meet emerging dilemmas. Climate disruption, pandemics, mass displacement, and algorithmic governance are present threats. Yet education often proceeds as if the future will mirror the past, updated with new devices. Students eager to prepare for tomorrow instead encounter yesterday's solutions, stripped of relevance. Carefully programmed pathways toward achievement falter when learners and institutions meet real complexity.

When learning is reduced to indoctrination, the pursuit of truth gives way to the preservation of power. Students receive orders instead of agency and freedom. Universities, too, risk silence when reputational or financial pressures outweigh academic freedom. When curiosity and courage are no longer nurtured, civic life narrows and the potential for self-actualization diminishes.

This raises a core question: *what is education for, if it cannot prepare people to defend truth, dignity, and the capacity to thrive together in this century?* Adding courses, layering devices, or outsourcing direction to markets does not resolve structural problems. These responses keep institutions running on life support while preventing renewal.

This book was nearly titled *No Hope Without Action*, after long conversations about what "hope" really means. Nietzsche (1996) called *hope* the cruelest evil, left in Pandora's jar to prolong human torment. Paulo Freire (1994) answered with *critical hope*, a hope tied to struggle and practice rather than passive waiting. Erich Fromm (1992) described hope as an active orientation, an inner readiness for the possible that resists passivity and insists on engagement. Between these views lies our concern: hope can sustain us, but without action it becomes an excuse for maintaining the *status quo*.

In moments like this, action cannot stay inside the lines. Institutions trained on compliance treat dissent as a defect and call it order. They absorb polite critique, then continue as before. If education is going to serve dignity, truth, and self-determination, we must refuse the practices that train obedience and build new ones in public. *We need a positive rebellion.*

Thus, this book's title leads us toward an answer to that question with an orientation and a method. *Build a Positive Rebellion* relates to a disciplined refusal of practices that harm, narrow, or disable people, paired with the work of constructing better options in public view, where learners, families, and communities can see, shape, and hold them accountable. *Positive* means constructive, grounded, and accountable to learners and communities. *Create New Education Futures* uses the plural form of "future" on purpose, because contexts differ and no single model should claim universal authority. We cannot know the future with certainty, but we can choose what guides us as we build our best futures.

And yet, hope endures. People cling to education because they still believe in its deeper promise: a shared practice of making meaning, building capacity, and shaping futures together. No other institution carries as much trust. The question is whether this promise can be recovered before the contradictions of the old model trigger collapse.

Identifying the problem is the first step. As this preface noted at its beginning, education is political. It produces inequality while promising mobility. It markets innovation while clinging to legacy paradigms. It invokes freedom while enforcing compliance. Superficial adjustments cannot resolve these tensions. Education must be redesigned to center lived experience, cultivate agency, and meet the demands of this century.

Redesign also requires a new relationship to knowledge. Information can be stored. Knowledge emerges when people make meaning and act on it. Systems that reward recall over understanding collapse these levels into one. The remedy is not to lower standards, but to move rigor elsewhere: ask real questions, wrestle with uncertainty, test models, publish work that matters, and revise in public. Rigor must be evidence-driven, but the evidence should reflect authentic learning (e.g., performances, prototypes, portfolios, impact), not narrow metrics.

Technology belongs in this redesign, but with purpose. Tools extend human capacities when they support modeling, design, collaboration, creation, and judgment. They distract when they automate judgment, reward spectacle, or surveil without trust.

Equity, planetary citizenship, and ecological realities must be built into education. Systems that reproduce predictable gaps by class, race, gender, language, or geography do so by design. Repair requires redesign: directing resources to sites of harm, amplifying marginalized knowledge, guiding admissions and placement, engaging families, and measuring belonging and growth rather than throughput.

Cultures of fear and control silence learners. Cultures of trust enable risk-taking. In institutions oriented toward trust, breaking rules becomes a discipline, not a reflex. Some rules safeguard equity or safety. Others persist to uphold habits that no longer serve learning. To break a rule responsibly requires naming the purpose it once served, the harm it now causes, and the standard that will replace it.

Manifesto 25 emerged as both a warning and a call to action. It rallies against schooling's architecture of fear, anxiety, and distrust that often hides behind standardization, compliance, and credentialism. The manifesto contains twenty-five principles for rethinking education in a world shaped by ecological disruption, accelerating technologies, widening inequities, and rising author-itarianism. These principles provide foundations for building better futures, especially in places where the right to self-determination is contested. They affirm that learning is a human right, that dignity and agency are requisites for growth, that technology must serve human and planetary purposes, and that equity and shared responsibility are essential for our well-being. Together, they offer a benchmark against which we can judge whether education meets this century's demands or retreats into the previous century's habits.

The aim of *Manifesto 25* is not to prescribe uniform solutions, but to anchor a shared orientation: principles communities can adapt, contest, and build upon in their own contexts. If we cannot know the future with certainty, we can still agree on what must guide us as we design it. Without such orientation, education drifts further behind, patching over crises instead of preparing us to meet them. With it, we have a compass for renewal.

This book is a companion to *Manifesto 25*. Each chapter explores one principle in greater depth, connects it with good practices, and offers guidance for action. These chapters are designed for non-sequential reading, allowing you to enter wherever the work meets your context; as you move across them, you will encounter recurring ideas that accumulate, sharpen, and test the same principles from different angles.

Interwoven throughout are two *intermezzos*: one collects the voices of youth confronting compliance in a world that demands agency; the other gathers reflections from signatories on where the freedom to learn is defended or constrained. Alongside these, *cahiers* (like the *Cahiers de Doléances* of the French Revolution), notebooks of ideas, grievances, and experiments, appear as spaces of testimony, critique, and design, extending the conversation beyond the text and into lived experience. The structure keeps us close to the principles while allowing practice and reflection to speak back.

This book is not a script. It offers tools and provocations. Use what helps. Set aside what does not. Add what your context requires. The manifesto calls for choices, not blind obedience. What will you defend? What will you retire? Where will you build?

The cracks in the old order are unmistakable. Whether they collapse into failure or open into renewal depends on decisions made now, in schools and ministries, in families and neighborhoods, in classrooms and councils. If education continues to manage appearances, it will keep losing trust. If it turns toward agency, meaning, equity, and planetary care, it can again become what people believe it should be: a practice of freedom, a craft of building futures, and a place where courage is learned and where rebellion becomes a form of love.

John W. Moravec
Minneapolis, Minnesota
April 2026

LET'S BUILD A POSITIVE REBELLION.

ENGAGE WITH
MANIFESTO25.ORG

Manifesto 25:
A framework for a positive rebellion in education

January 1, 2025

Our education systems are failing to meet the needs of a rapidly changing world. Systems designed to solve problems of the past perpetuate inequities, stifle creativity, and fail to prepare learners for the complexity and uncertainty of today and tomorrow. Ten years ago, *Manifesto 15* called for bold action to reimagine learning for a changing world. Since then, the rhetoric has grown louder, but very little has changed. Legacy philosophies continue to fail to meet the demands of our present and future.

This document presents a framework, through a set of principles, to cure the inertia and complacency that have held learners back. We seek to dismantle outdated paradigms, challenge entrenched power structures, and address the systemic issues that perpetuate inequity, limit potential, and stifle innovation. We aim to inspire the creation of dynamic, inclusive, and learner-centered ecosystems that equip *all* individuals to thrive as full participants in an interconnected world.

Hope is not enough. Action must replace rhetoric. Waiting for reforms and polite conversations cannot address the urgency of this moment. This document is a call for a *positive rebellion*. It urges us to collaborate in dismantling outdated paradigms, creating new ones, and co-designing an education system that serves all learners, unlocks human potential, and equips us not only to survive, but thrive, in a world beyond our imagination. This starts by coming together to empower learners at the core.

Our way forward requires courage, creativity, and community. We must reimagine education as a dynamic force that equips every learner to shape a thriving, equitable, and sustainable world.

WHAT WE HAVE LEARNED SO FAR

1.   **"The future is already here—it's just not very evenly distributed" (William Gibson in Gladstone, 1998).**
     The field of education lags behind other industries because it focuses on the past rather than the future. We teach the history of literature but ignore the future of storytelling. We emphasize traditional mathematical concepts but neglect the creation of new mathematics to shape tomorrow. What is labeled as 'revolutionary' in education has already occurred in fragmented, localized ways. To realize meaningful change, we must learn from these scattered efforts, share experiences, and take the necessary risks to embrace a forward-looking approach in our practice.

2.   **1.0 schools cannot teach 3.0, 4.0, 5.0 ... kids.**
     In other words, schools designed for the industrial age cannot meet the needs of a digital, interconnected era. We need to redefine and build a clear understanding of *what* we are educating for, *why* we do it, and *for whom* our educational systems serve. Mainstream compulsory schooling is based on an outdated, 19th-century model for creating citizens with the potential to become obedient factory workers and bureaucrats. In the post-industrial and increasingly digital era, this should no longer be the end goal of education. We need to support learners to become innovators, capable of leveraging their own imagination and creativity to realize new outcomes for society. We do this because today's challenges cannot be solved through old thinking. And we are all co-responsible for creating futures with positive outcomes that benefit all people in the world.

3.   **Kids are people, too.**
     All students must be treated and respected as human beings with recognized, universal human rights and responsibilities. This means students must have an active say in the choices regarding

their learning, including how their schools are run, how and when they learn, and all other areas of everyday life. This is inclusion in a real sense. Students of all ages must be afforded liberties to pursue educational opportunities and approaches for learning that are appropriate for them, as long as their decisions do not infringe on the liberties of others to do the same (adapted from EUDEC, 2023).

4. **Schools must be havens of uncommon safety and extraordinary respect.**
Social-emotional and relational intelligence must be at the core, beyond test scores and rigid academics, fostering empathy, self-awareness, and constructive conflict resolution. The opportunity to be vulnerable in a safe space allows for genuine, authentic connections with others and oneself. In this way, schools establish the interpersonal foundation learners need to navigate diverse perspectives and thrive in an interconnected world. These intelligences are not optional; they are the cornerstone of personal growth and collective progress.

5. **Authentic learning comes from freedom, not from being pushed into a predetermined path.**
The traditional top-down, teacher-student model suppresses curiosity and erodes intrinsic motivation, reducing learning to compliance exercises. Instead, we must adopt flat, collaborative approaches that value peer learning, peer teaching, and distributed responsibility. Educators must create environments where students can decide when and how to take their leaps, knowing that failure is not an endpoint but a natural step in the learning process. Failing is a natural part of learning where we can always try again. In a flat learning environment, the teacher's role is to help make sure the learner makes a well-balanced decision. Failing is part of the path of learning, but the creation of failures is not.

6.   **Learning together, teaching together.**
      Education thrives when everyone becomes both a teacher and
      a learner. By breaking free from artificial age silos, schools can
      evolve into vibrant hubs where children, parents, elders, and
      community members exchange skills, insights, and creativity as
      open knowledge and networking ecosystems. Older students
      mentor younger peers while gaining fresh perspectives, and
      parents and community leaders bring real-world knowledge,
      enriched by the curiosity of children. This dynamic, reciprocal
      process celebrates intergenerational wisdom, strengthens social
      bonds, and empowers all to shape a meaningful future.

7.   **Learning occurs in ecosystems, not boxes.**
      Rigid schedules and siloed classrooms reduce education to a
      transactional process, ignoring its lifelong, interwoven nature.
      Formal schooling should be one strand in a wider tapestry of
      experiences that involves family, community, workplaces, and
      digital networks. By blending these contexts, we erase bound-
      aries between formal and informal learning, allowing knowledge
      and skills to circulate freely. In such environments, students learn
      to adapt to various roles, work across generations, and embrace
      insights from unexpected sources. Freed from the confines of
      boxes, education fuels curiosity and self-confidence, preparing
      learners to flourish in an ever-evolving world.

8.   **Nirvana is found in the fusion of agency with self-efficacy.**
      When learners and educators achieve both agency (the freedom
      to shape their paths) and self-efficacy (the belief that they can
      succeed) education transcends traditional goals and reaches
      its ultimate purpose: empowering individuals to lead fulfilling,
      impactful lives. Schools should actively cultivate this balance by
      blending choice-driven learning with consistent opportunities
      for learners to build and demonstrate competence. This fusion
      prepares students for the future by enabling the inspiration and
      vision necessary to create it.

9. **Educators are creators, collaborators, and innovators, not cogs in a machine.**
    Reducing them to implementers of legacy methods undermines both learners and the future of education. To address the demands of a dynamic, interconnected world, educators must be valued as individuals with unique needs, aspirations, and creative potential. Transforming education means enabling educators as co-creators, equipping them with trust, tools, and resources to drive innovation. Recognizing educators as professionals and partners fosters thriving learning environments where both teachers and students flourish, inspiring curiosity, adaptability, and resilience.

10. **Don't value what we measure; measure what we value.**
    Assessments should empower learners, not instill fear. The obsession with high-stakes testing abets anxiety and reduces education to rote memorization, sidelining critical thinking and problem-solving. The cult of high-stakes testing has become the misguided arbiters of success, spreading a harmful culture of comparison and underperformance anxiety worldwide. This fixation undermines genuine innovation, with promising ideas dismissed due to measurement concerns. Worse, schools produce leaders ill-equipped to interpret data critically. We must eliminate compulsory high-stakes testing and redirect resources toward initiatives that advance authentic learning and mean-ingful, multidimensional growth.

11. **Bad use of technology is a symptom, not the problem.**
    Technology is not a solution by itself, but when used thoughtfully, it can unlock new ways of learning and creating. We must move beyond old practices and truly harness technology as a tool for transformation, rather than obsessing over the latest tools while neglecting their potential to drive change. Swapping blackboards for smartboards or books for tablets while clinging to old teaching methods is like building a nuclear plant to power a horse cart:

wasteful and ineffective. Yet, nothing has changed, and we still focus tremendous resources on these tools and squander our opportunities to exploit their potential to transform *what* we learn and *how* we do it. By recreating practices of the past with technologies, schools focus more on managing hardware and software rather than developing students' *mindware* and the *purposive* use of these tools.

12. **Learning happens if we attend to it or not.**
    Most learning is 'invisible.' It occurs outside formal instruction through informal, serendipitous experiences. It happens through curiosity, experimentation, and unplanned experiences; more like breathing than deliberate effort. Rather than forcing invisible learning into visibility, we should focus on creating environments that trust and nurture its organic flow. This means nurturing workplaces, schools, and communities that value exploration, provide opportunities to seek knowledge, and respect that not all learning needs to be measured or reported. By allowing learning to remain unseen, we preserve its authenticity and permit individuals to grow in ways that are meaningful to them. Trust, not surveillance, is the true driver of innovation and growth.

13. **Knowledge is constructed from meaning, not management.**
    When we talk about knowledge and innovation, we frequently commingle or confuse the concepts with data and information instead. Too often, we fool ourselves into thinking that we give learners 'knowledge' when we are just testing them for the rote recall of information. To be clear: Data are bits and pieces here and there, from which we combine into information. Knowledge is about taking information and creating meaning at a personal level. We innovate when we take action with what we know to create new value. Understanding this difference exposes one of the greatest problems facing school management and teaching:

While we are good at managing information, we simply cannot manage the knowledge in students' heads without degrading it back to information.

14. **Standardization kills creativity and innovation.**
One-size-fits-all education turns learners into uniform outputs, measuring success through narrow assessments. By fragmenting knowledge into isolated subjects, it overlooks the complexity of real-world challenges and curbs experimentation and bold thinking. To foster genuine innovation, we must abandon rigid uniformity and adopt adaptive, learner-centered approaches that emphasize open-ended inquiry and interdisciplinary collaboration. Only when students can explore their interests, exchange diverse perspectives, and engage in authentic problem-solving does true creativity flourish.

15. **Knowledge grows where the boundaries of networks intersect.**
The emerging pedagogy of this century isn't carefully planned—it evolves fluidly. Learning unfolds as we traverse and expand networks, connecting individual knowledge to create new understandings. By sharing experiences, we generate social knowledge that enriches collective insight. Education must prioritize equipping individuals with the tools, competencies, and literacies (such as digital fluency, cultural awareness, and network navigation) needed to thrive in these interconnected systems. Through this process, learners contextualize their unique talents and knowledge, empowering them to tackle new challenges with creativity and confidence.

16. **Degrees are obsolete by design.**
Many static degree programs, designed for fixed fields with clear endpoints, are outdated or obsolete before students even finish their first year. Traditional diplomas fail to keep up with accelerating change and often do not capture the depth of real-world

skills and achievements. A concerted shift toward a new, decentralized system is needed that values creativity, problem-solving, and real impact over time spent in a classroom. Learners need dynamic recognition systems that adapt with them, rewarding growth and contributions that reflect the ever-changing demands of the world.

17.   **Any education system that tolerates inequities is complicit in injustice.**

Systems designed to perpetuate inequality fail everyone. Schools must move beyond token acknowledgments of diversity to dismantle systemic barriers. Curricula should amplify marginalized voices and ensure that every learner is genuinely seen, heard, and valued. Equity and inclusion are not optional add-ons—they are the foundation of a fair and sustainable education system.

18.   **Acts of global citizenship transform personal experience into planetary impact.**

Rooted in local contexts and meaningful engagement with diverse communities, it bridges individual perspectives with global challenges. Education must equip learners to tackle these challenges through cross-cultural empathy, ethical responsibility, and collaborative problem-solving. This requires planetary-focused literacies—frameworks that connect local actions to global solutions while respecting individual and collective rights. By aligning personal agency with shared tools, education empowers learners to act locally and globally, shaping sustainable and equitable futures.

19.   **The future belongs to nerds, geeks, makers, dreamers, and knowmads.**

While not everybody will or should become an entrepreneur, those who do not develop entrepreneurial skills are at a great disadvantage. Our education systems should focus on the development of *entreprenerds*: individuals who leverage their specialized knowledge to dream, create, make, explore, learn, and promote entrepreneurial, cultural, or social endeavors, taking risks and enjoying the process as much as the final outcome, without fearing the potential failures or mistakes that the journey includes.

20. **Reality is not optional.**

Ignoring our shared reality is a collapse into chaos. Weaponized postmodernism, where facts are twisted and accountability evaded, threatens the foundation of education and society itself. Shared realities are not optional; without them, critical thinking fails, trust evaporates, and collaboration becomes impossible. Education must confront distortion head-on, rooting itself in empirical evidence while unleashing our imaginations to solve new challenges. To build a sustainable future, learners must be equipped to challenge distortions, reject evasion of accountability, and navigate complexity with intellectual courage.

21. **An education that ignores the planet is an education without a future.**

With climate catastrophe looming, any curriculum that neglects environmental stewardship is both deficient and irresponsible. Education must actively shape students' futures and the world around them. Learners should not passively study the environment; they must be empowered as co-creators of solutions and active guardians of the planet. By enabling students with future-ready skills and agency to address grand challenges, and integrating planetary-focused literacies into a dynamic, flexible learning process, we foster innovation and a personal connection to sustainability that inspires lasting impact.

22.   **We *can* and *must* build cultures of trust in our schools and communities.**

As long as our education systems continue to be based on fear, anxiety, and distrust, challenges to all of the above will persist. If educators are to build a collective capacity to transform education, we need engaged communities, and we also need to engage with the communities we serve. This requires a new theory of action, centered on trust, where students, schools, governments, businesses, parents, and communities may engage in collaborative initiatives to co-create new education futures.

23.   **Break the rules, but understand *why* clearly first.**

Our school systems are built on cultures of obedience, enforced compliance, and complacency. The creativity of students, staff, and our institutions is inherently stultified. It is easier to be told what to think than to think for ourselves. Openly asking questions and building a metacognitive awareness of what we have created and what we would like to do about it can best cure this institutionalized malaise. Only then can we engineer justified breaks from the system that challenge the *status quo* and have the potential to create real impact.

24.   **Activism is a space where unlearning thrives.**

Whether through non-violent civil disobedience, street protests, artistic demonstrations, or performative resistance, activism challenges the *status quo* and rebuilds from the ground up. It teaches resilience, agency, and the courage to confront broken systems, including education itself. Educators must embrace activism as a core learning tool, transforming passive learners into active participants in shaping the world.

25. **Question everything.**

Start with this manifesto. Blind acceptance breeds complacency. As co-learners, we must provide safe spaces to critically evaluate all ideas, including the ones presented here. By contributing to a culture of critical thinking and open dialogue, the development of one's self-awareness is encouraged and individuals are enabled to contribute toward a continuous evolution of how we teach and learn.

The challenges in education persist because they threaten entrenched power and disrupt the *status quo*. For centuries, truths that challenge privilege (whether heliocentrism, the validity of evolutionary biology, or the reality of human-driven climate change) have faced resistance. Education, similarly constrained by antiquated priorities, demands not more awareness, but the courage to dismantle barriers, reject complacency, and build systems that serve every learner and community.

No one can do this alone. A movement for learning futures demands a coalition of educators, learners, families, policymakers, and communities. By uniting our unique strengths, we can dismantle outdated systems, redesign curricula, and create environments where equity, creativity, and curiosity thrive. Each action we take counts, whether reimagining how we teach, fostering cultures of trust within schools, or advocating for policy change that centers learning as a lifelong right.

Together, we can create an education system that empowers every learner to thrive in an unpredictable world. It's time to act boldly, collectively, and with purpose.

THE FUTURE IS HERE.
WHAT WE BUILD TODAY MATTERS.

We are

John Moravec (principal author, USA), **Gustavo Andrade** (Mexico), **Chris Bagley** (UK), **Constanze Beyer** (Germany), **Paola Boccia** (Argentina/Germany), **Edwin De Bree** (Netherlands), **Vivian Breucker** (Germany), **Alexandra Castro Ferrada** (USA), **María Mercedes Civarolo** (Spain/Argentina), **Cristóbal Cobo** (Chile), **Antonio L. Delgado Pérez** (USA), **Claudia Dikmans** (Germany), **Albus Duc Hoang** (Vietnam), **Kristina House** (Canada), **Silvia Enriquez** (Argentina), **Martine Eyzenga** (Netherlands), **Tomas C. Ferber** (Germany), **Richard Fransham** (Canada), **Gustavo Garcia Lutz** (Uruguay), **Peter Gray** (USA), **Christel Hartkamp** (Netherlands), **Pekka Ihanainen** (Finland), **Marcel Kampman** (Netherlands), **Bob Kartous** (Czech Republic), **Kateřina Kolínková** (Czech Republic), **Kamila Koutná** (Czech Republic), **Florian Kretzschmar** (Germany), **Nicola Kriesel** (Germany), **Luis R. Lara** (Argentina), **Diego Leal** (Colombia), **Carlos Lizárraga Celaya** (USA), **María Cristina Martínez-Bravo** (Ecuador), **Juraj Mazák** (Slovakia), **Alejandra Mendoza Garza** (Mexico), **Farid Mokhtar Noriega** (Spain), **María Mercedes Moravec** (USA), **Daniel Navarrete** (Colombia), **Varlei Xavier Nogueira** (Brazil), **Alejandro Núñez Urquijo** (Colombia), **Hugo Pardo Kuklinski** (Argentina/Spain), **Alejandro Pisanty** (Mexico), **Lucas Potenza** (Argentina), **Noemi Pulido** (Argentina), **Luis Napoleón Quintanilla** (El Salvador), **Dinant Roode** (Netherlands), **Javier José Simon** (Argentina), **Alison Snieckus** (USA), **Max Ugaz** (Peru), **Paloma Valdivia Vizarreta** (Spain), **David Vidal** (Spain), **Evangelos Vlachakis** (Greece), **Tim Weinert** (Germany), **Monika Wernz** (Germany), and **Alex Wiedemann** (Germany).

1
Building futures we cannot yet imagine

Education teaches yesterday to children who will live in tomorrow. While medicine rewrites genomes and technology engineers intelligence, schools remain anchored to the past. Literature courses rehearse the canon but overlook the future of storytelling in podcasts, interactive fiction, and virtual worlds. Mathematics still prizes manual techniques while sidelining climate modeling, data science, and artificial intelligence. Innovation elsewhere races ahead. Education drags its feet.

This backwardness is intentional. Schools are designed to be conservative institutions. They valorize stability, continuity, and predictability, precisely the qualities that industries outside of education now abandon in order to survive. In technology, companies fold, pivot, or reinvent themselves in the span of a few years. In medicine, therapies are trialed, refined, and deployed on timescales once unimaginable. Agriculture reorganizes its entire supply chains in response to climate disruption. Education, in contrast, insists on shielding itself from change, preferring curricula written decades ago and practices that promise control rather than creativity (Tyack & Cuban, 1995).

Meanwhile, the ground beneath us is shifting faster than schools can respond. Futures most of us cannot yet imagine are taking shape through artificial intelligence, biotechnology, quantum computing, climate disruption, and upheavals still unnamed. These forces do not wait for the approval of ministries or accreditation bodies. They reshape work, culture, politics, and knowledge production in real time.

Artificial intelligence generates text, images, and scientific hypotheses at scales that would have sounded absurd five years ago. Biotechnologies allow us to edit genomes, manufacture organs, and alter ecosystems. Quantum computing may crack problems in chemistry, finance, and logistics that overwhelm today's machines. These breakthroughs carry both the promise of flourishing and the risk of collapse. They open paths toward techno-utopias and toward nightmares.

Preparing students for this world requires more than transmitting established knowledge. It requires foresight, adaptability, ethical judgment, and the courage to invent what does not yet exist. A graduate fluent only in prescribed knowledge is not simply underprepared. They are disarmed in a century defined by uncertainty (UNESCO, 2021). Schools cannot remain passive. They must train learners to read emerging patterns, improvise solutions, and co-create futures that are inclusive, just, and worth living in.

From _Manifesto 25_:

"The future is already here — it's just not evenly distributed"
–William Gibson (interviewed in Gladstone, 1998). The field of education lags behind other industries because it focuses on the past rather than the future. We teach the history of literature but ignore the future of storytelling. We emphasize traditional mathematical concepts but neglect the creation of new mathematics to shape tomorrow. What is labeled as 'revolutionary' in education has already occurred in fragmented, localized ways. To realize meaningful change, we must learn from these scattered efforts, share experiences, and take the necessary risks to embrace a forward-looking approach in our practice.

The uneven distribution of the future extends beyond innovation in teaching and learning. It reflects deep inequities in educational opportunity. Students from historically marginalized backgrounds often lack access to emerging technologies and future-focused curricula, limiting their ability to engage with, or shape, the futures we claim to seek.

This gap restricts their capacity not only to understand emerging ideas, but to participate in creating and defining them. The future then risks being designed by a privileged few, reproducing existing inequities by new means (van Dijk, 2020). If we want a future that is accessible and inclusive, educational institutions must prioritize equitable access to future-oriented learning opportunities. Schools and policymakers should deliberately provide learners with access to advanced technology, digital platforms, experiences, and *mindware*, software of the mind, that supports imaginative thinking and original solutions. Addressing uneven distribution also means cultivating the belief, in students and educators alike, that they have a role in designing our futures.

BREAKING INNOVATIONS FROM ISOLATION

A backward-looking approach trains institutions to watch innovation from a distance. Schools isolate themselves from change rather than adopting or developing it. Yet educators and institutions around the world are experimenting: students learn storytelling through augmented and virtual reality, explore mathematics through computational modeling, and engage interdisciplinary projects centered on sustainability, public health, and digital citizenship. These efforts rarely move beyond local pockets because systemic support is thin and the exchange of practice is fragmented.

Even where digital tools are widespread, schools often use them to replicate traditional methods. Interactive platforms and virtual reality re-enact historical events or familiar narratives instead of supporting new forms of storytelling and original creation. Computational modeling and AI are used to reinforce existing mathematics rather than to generate insight or tackle unsolved challenges. Technology then becomes a veneer of modernization rather than a shift in what learning makes possible (Zhao, 2018; Kirschner & De Bruyckere, 2017). Students' capacity for innovation remains untapped.

And still, sparks exist. Around the world, educators and students are building new methods of learning that challenge the limits of traditional schooling. These efforts prove that alternatives are imaginable and already underway. Yet they remain fragile. Many depend on the passion of a few teachers, the tolerance of a sympathetic administrator, or the short-term lift of a grant. Without systemic support, they flare and fade.

The lesson is plain. Innovation cannot remain a hobby or a passive side project. When schools treat future-oriented practice as peripheral, they guarantee it will wither in isolation. To matter, innovation must be central to education's purpose, resourced, shared, and scaled with care.

Schools and policymakers can begin by identifying, evaluating, and expanding promising innovations. Teachers need structured opportunities to collaborate and share what they learn from experimentation. Professional development and school culture must reward risk-taking and forward-thinking. Policy must back this work with resources and recognize innovation as central to teacher and school evaluation, not an extracurricular option.

MORE THAN GADGETS AND TESTS

So what would it mean to take the future as seriously as the past? Not another gadget in the classroom. Not another standardized test. It would mean practices that build the capacities every learner will need in a century of uncertainty.

Our key starting point is *futures literacy*: helping learners explore alternative scenarios and recognize the drivers shaping change. Students map what could happen and ask what futures they would prefer. The work prepares rather than predicts (Miller, 2018). It builds the foresight and agility to improvise under uncertainty.

Equally important are opportunities to tackle complex, cross-disciplinary challenges. Instead of working within subject silos, students engage problems such as climate disruption, cybersecurity, and migration, where no single discipline offers sufficient answers. They learn to integrate diverse knowledge systems, weigh ethical tradeoffs, and collaborate across boundaries. The most urgent problems of the century will not arrive labeled "math" or "literature." They will demand hybrid, creative forms of problem-solving.

Hands-on work with emerging technologies is another pathway. Robotics, artificial intelligence, virtual reality, and biotechnology are not just tools for industry. They are terrains where values and futures are contested. When learners experiment directly with these technologies, they build technical confidence and ethical awareness. They become creators and critics, not passive consumers.

Education must also cultivate entrepreneurial imagination: the capacity to see possibilities where others see limits. This is not a mandate for every student to launch a start-up. It is about resilience, initiative, and the courage to turn ideas into action. Paired with opportunities for global collaboration through digital exchanges or transnational projects, learners can practice negotiating across cultures, time zones, and worldviews. They begin to understand that shaping the future is a collective enterprise.

A future-oriented curriculum aligns knowledge and skill with both anticipated and unforeseen shifts. It expands what counts as core learning. Digital literacy, interactive media, biotechnology, digital citizenship, and applied mathematics for real-world challenges become central. Practical experience, interdisciplinary projects, and ongoing engagement with emerging technologies move from enrichment to expectation. The goal is readiness to navigate change and contribute to shaping it.

THE FUTURES WE FACE

We stand at a threshold. Education can keep embalming the past, producing graduates fluent in obsolete knowledge, and watch as the future is designed without them. Or it can claim its true role: preparing people not only to survive the future, but to shape it.

The tools, knowledge, and imagination to do this are already in our hands. Every moment of delay steals possibility from those who will inherit the balance of this century. The choice is stark: complicity in reproducing a dead world, or participation in building futures we cannot yet imagine. If we refuse to act, we condemn another generation to study a world already gone. If we act, we open the future to everyone. Education must stop rehearsing yesterday and start building tomorrow.

2

1.0 schools cannot teach 3.0, 4.0, 5.0 ... kids

In one classroom, a student copies notes about a centuries-old war. Outside school, that same student builds game mods, edits videos for social media, and debates politics in global online forums. Another student memorizes formulas without context, even as they help manage a family budget shaped by inflation, housing insecurity, and climate-related disruption.

These scenes reveal a widening disconnect between school and life. While classrooms demand obedience to fixed curricula, students navigate complex social and technological systems that require adaptability, judgment, and creativity. As this gap widens, schools drift away from what matters most to learners, weakening both relevance and purpose.

Education systems worldwide remain anchored in designs rooted in the nineteenth century. Most schools still operate according to an industrial, "1.0" logic: producing obedient workers and compliant citizens for factory economies. Uniform schedules, teacher-centered instruction, and standardized assessment reflect this inheritance. These structures once served a historical function. They no longer align with a digital, interconnected, rapidly changing world.

The labels 1.0, 2.0, and 3.0 draw from a framework introduced in *Knowmad Society* (Moravec, 2013). Education 1.0 mirrors the industrial model, centered on compliance and information delivery. Education 2.0 introduces limited learner-centered approaches but remains teacher-directed. Education 3.0 shifts toward co-creation, networked learning, and participatory culture. As we accelerate toward 4.0 and 5.0 futures, marked by artificial intelligence, ecological disruption, and global interdependence, schools must move beyond passive transmission and industrial skill formation to become platforms for innovation, collaboration, and creativity. These generational metaphors, reflected in *Manifesto 25*, represent how society evolves across technological and cultural waves. while most schools remain stuck in the old paradigm:

From *Manifesto 25*:

> *1.0 schools cannot teach 3.0, 4.0, 5.0 ... kids. In other words, schools designed for the industrial age cannot meet the needs of a digital, interconnected era. We need to redefine and build a clear understanding of **what** we are educating for, **why** we do it, and **for whom** our educational systems serve. Mainstream compulsory schooling is based on an outdated, 19th-century model for creating citizens with the potential to become obedient factory workers and bureaucrats. In the post-industrial and increasingly digital era, this should no longer be the end goal of education. We need to support learners to become innovators, capable of leveraging their own imagination and creativity to realize new outcomes for society. We do this because today's challenges cannot be solved through old thinking. And we are all co-responsible for creating futures with positive outcomes that benefit all people in the world.*

TODAY'S LEARNERS, TOMORROW'S CHALLENGES

Many of today's students grow up in a hyperconnected world, shaped by digital ecosystems, participatory media, and instantaneous access to global knowledge. They form identities across multiple platforms, navigate overlapping cultures, and collaborate with peers in real-time across geographic boundaries. Their daily lives require adaptability, systems thinking, and creativity. They are expected to address complex global challenges (i.e., climate instability, political polarization, technological disruption) without the tools to make sense of a world that defies easy answers. While society demands that they be innovators, leaders, and problem-solvers, school often prepares them for roles and structures that no longer exist.

Yet the structure and culture of schooling remain tied to static curricula, rigid schedules, and assessment systems optimized for recall and routine rather than insight and invention. The gap between what students need and what schools provide continues to grow, exacerbated by technological acceleration and societal complexity. Classrooms often remain disconnected from the dynamic worlds students inhabit outside school, leaving many learners unchallenged, uninspired, or underserved. The cost is real: disengagement, lost potential, and a failure to prepare the next generation to lead meaningful change.

Moving forward requires a shift in purpose. Education can no longer prioritize memorization and compliance. It must cultivate imagination, critical thinking, ethical judgment, collaboration, and the capacity to generate novel responses to emerging problems. Learners must be supported as active creators of knowledge and shapers of the future, not passive recipients of information (Fullan, Quinn, & McEachen, 2018).

This shift begins with two questions: *what are we educating for? And, for whose benefit?* Too often, education systems serve labor markets, political interests, and dominant cultural narratives rather than learners. Schools were built to sort, control, and discipline. They prepare students to occupy predefined roles, not to question or redesign them.

JUST 'SMART ENOUGH' TO BE OBEDIENTLY USEFUL

As George Carlin (2005) brutally put it, the aim of education is to produce workers "just smart enough to run the machines," but "just dumb enough to passively accept these increasingly shittier jobs." His words captured a deliberate strategy to engineer compliance and suppress critical thought. The machines that once defined factory work have largely been replaced by algorithms, automation, and distributed systems. Yet the logic of control and efficiency still shapes how schools function today. And to who's benefit?

This industrial model treats students as inputs in a production line: they are processed, measured, and outputted based on standardized benchmarks. Uniformity is rewarded. Deviation is penalized. Imagination is often considered disruptive. The result is an education system that suppresses curiosity in favor of order, and favors technical competency over ethical imagination. We may no longer train students to operate machines, but we continue to shape them to fit within the machinery of compliance. This is profoundly misaligned with the demands of our era.

FOR WHOM SHOULD EDUCATION SERVE?

If we take seriously what we know about learners, society, and the scale of challenges ahead, education systems built on standardization and sorting are no longer sufficient. The aim cannot be employability alone. Education must support shared survival, democratic renewal, and collective capacity to shape equitable futures. It determines whose voices count, whose knowledge matters, and whose futures are possible. To meet this responsibility, education must equip all learners to navigate uncertainty, act with ethical imagination, and participate fully in a world defined by interdependence.

The current system privileges dominant norms while marginalizing students whose languages, cultures, and lived experiences fall outside the mainstream. These exclusions are maintained by design. Reimagining education requires naming this reality and committing to a different future. That future centers historically marginalized learners, educators, families, and communities as partners in decision-making. Education must be built with learners, not imposed on them, grounded in agency, dignity, and shared ownership.

REIMAGINING SCHOOL STRUCTURES

If schools are to remain relevant, they must abandon the factory floor. This means rethinking organization, time, space, and authority. A 1.0 model relies on standardization, siloed disciplines, bell schedules, and passive instruction. It rewards recall and test performance and structures learning into rigid units of time.

By contrast, schools grounded in 3.0 and beyond are learner-centered, adaptive, and networked. They support agency through co-designed pathways and organize learning around meaningful questions and real challenges. Teachers act as facilitators and co-learners. Students engage problems that demand creativity, collaboration, and critical thought across disciplines.

Time and space become flexible. Learners collaborate across age groups, pursue long-term projects, and connect with peers and mentors globally. Rows of desks give way to studios, labs, and community spaces. Assessment shifts toward portfolios, exhibitions, and reflection. Success is measured by growth, insight, and the ability to communicate learning with clarity and purpose.

In these environments, technology empowers rather than monitors. It connects learners across cultures, expands access to knowledge, and supports creative expression. It builds digital literacy, systems thinking, media fluency, and ethical reasoning. These capacities are essential for addressing the challenges ahead and shaping just, sustainable outcomes.

Shifting from 1.0 to 3.0 and beyond must go beyond a surface-level reform, demanding a complete redesign of the *space* in which schools function, from how *time* is structured, to what is learned, to *how* learning is assessed. This new system must prioritize flexibility, collaboration, and relevance, supporting student agency and connection to real-world challenges. It should be built to prepare learners for a world defined by rapid change, uncertainty, and interdependence.

We cannot address today's challenges with yesterday's tools. Education must be redesigned around the realities we face and the futures we intend to build. That requires confronting institutional inertia and committing to systemic change, not symbolic gestures. The choice is between redesign and decay.

The gap between yesterday's schools and today's realities is now too wide to ignore. Bridging it means asking harder questions. Does this policy disrupt outdated systems or reinforce them? Does this design cultivate imagination, collaboration, and relevance, or does it preserve compliance and control? If it ties us to the past, it should be abandoned. Education must become a space of open design, not a closed factory, where learners are prepared not only to succeed in the future, but to shape it on their own terms.

3
Kids are people, too

Most schools are built on control. Students are told when to sit, when to speak, what to study, and how to behave. They are ranked, sorted, and measured, often without being asked what they think. Adults decide *what* counts as learning and *how* it happens. Young people live with the consequences. That's a problem.

Young people are citizens from birth, not apprentices to adulthood. They are most affected by education policy, curriculum decisions, and school rules, yet they usually have the least power to shape them. As stakeholders in both school and society, they deserve a meaningful role in shaping their learning and their futures. The challenges they will face, ecological collapse, social fragmentation, rapid technological change, demand agency rooted in respect and trust.

Many barriers to student agency are built into the structure of schooling. Standardized testing narrows curriculum and constrains teacher and student choice, sending a clear message: what counts is what can be measured. In many countries, legal frameworks treat students as passive recipients of instruction rather than rights-bearing individuals with a say in their education. Even where participation is encouraged, cultural assumptions about childhood, especially the belief that young people lack the maturity or judgment to contribute meaningfully, undermine real inclusion. These obstacles reflect deeper values about power and whose voice matters. Until they change, efforts at "student voice" will remain cosmetic. Authentic change requires dismantling systems that deny students the ability to shape their own learning.

From *Manifesto 25*:

> ***Kids are people, too.*** *All students must be treated and respected as human beings with recognized, universal human rights and responsibilities. This means students must have an active say in the choices regarding their learning, including how their schools are run, how and when they learn, and all other areas of everyday life. This is inclusion in a real sense. Students of all ages must be afforded liberties to pursue educational opportunities and approaches for learning that are appropriate for them, as long as their decisions do not infringe on the liberties of others to do the same (adapted from EUDEC, 2023).*

INCLUSION AS SHARED POWER AND RESPONSIBILITY

Inclusion about participation, not presence. Typically, "student voice" is reduced to token surveys, scripted forums, or assignments where the format is open but the outcome is predetermined. These token gestures mask the top-down nature of school decision-making and give the illusion of inclusion without shifting any real power.

Students should have a hand in shaping curriculum, timetables, discipline policies, and all facets of school governance. This is already in practice around the world:

- **In Finland**, many schools practice student democracy through structured class meetings, student-led initiatives, and integration of student councils into school governance. Participation is built into the culture, not bolted on as an afterthought.
- **In India**, organizations such as Shikshantar have supported unschooling and learner-directed models that respect children as capable decision-makers. Learners co-design their days, pursue community-based projects, and document their learning journeys without grades or rigid timetables.
- **Throughout Europe**, democratic schools within the European Democratic Education Community operate on principles where students

and staff share equal voting rights on all matters, from budgeting to curriculum to staffing.

- **In South Africa**, the Equal Education movement mobilized students to speak up about school conditions, infrastructure, and inequality, effectively pushing for policy change by elevating youth voices in national education debates.

What happens when we place more trust in kids? *They turn out just fine.* When students co-create the structures and rhythms of school life, the outcomes can be durable. A 2024 study of Sudbury-type schools (Hartkamp-Bakker & Martens, 2024) found that students exercising real choice developed stronger self-determination, motivation, and ownership over their lives. They reported deeper confidence and a clearer sense of personal responsibility. More broadly, research on democratic and learner-directed schooling suggests that when students help shape their environments, they engage more fully, take initiative, and develop negotiation, collaboration, and accountability through lived experience. Being heard, and being responsible, teaches belonging and prepares young people to contribute to their communities.

RESPONSIBILITY AS LIVED LEARNING EXPERIENCES

A rights-based approach includes responsibilities. But responsibility is not something adults impose. It is something communities build and agree to together. Students learn responsibility through resolving conflicts, setting shared norms, managing group work, co-creating school priorities, caring for learning environments, and even through free play (Gray, 2023). When students are partners rather than subjects, accountability becomes mutual. Schools become less about managing behavior and more about nurturing contribution and belonging.

Sudbury Valley School in Massachusetts offers a concrete example of inclusion through shared power and responsibility. At Sudbury, students of all ages have equal voting rights with staff on school rules, hiring, and governance.

There is no imposed curriculum, no grading system, and no compulsory classes. Students direct their learning, whether that means music composition, programming, painting, or long conversations with peers. Governance happens through democratic assemblies and student-run judicial committees, where even a six-year-old can hold a fifteen-year-old accountable. Shared power is practiced daily.

In Peru, the Escuela Democrática de Huamachuco, formed in partnership with the Kapriole school in Freiburg, Germany, adapts democratic education to local Andean traditions and a commitment to environmental awareness and human rights. Students participate in weekly assemblies to propose and vote on school matters, from schedules and curriculum themes to conflict resolution. There are no formal grades. Learning is guided by student interests, community needs, and collective agreements. Responsibility is lived: students organize clean-up rotations, co-facilitate workshops, and help manage school resources. The work fosters autonomy, mutual respect, and civic responsibility grounded in local culture.

These outcomes become possible when schools treat students as people whose voices shape their educational lives, not as subjects to be managed. But realizing these rights requires more than changing attitudes. It requires questioning schedules, grading systems, discipline policies, and the assumption that adults always know best. It requires dismantling structural barriers that codify compliance as normal.

In many systems, student rights are constrained by policies and norms that privilege standardization and control. High-stakes testing narrows curriculum and reduces students to test-takers. Legal frameworks limit decision-making power, from governance to discipline. Cultural assumptions about childhood compound the problem by framing young people as too naïve to participate in decisions that shape their lives. Breaking these barriers requires redesign grounded in two principles: respect and trust.

STARTING WITH RESPECT AND TRUST

All people are entitled to basic human rights, including young people. Children and youth are protected under the *UN Convention on the Rights of the Child*, including the right to be heard in decisions that affect them, the right to education that supports their development and well-being, and the right to freedom of thought and expression.

Yet schools built on control often ignore these rights. Respect should not depend on age or obedience. It should be the minimum we expect from each other. Students deserve systems that presume capability, support agency, and invite participation.

Agency enables purpose. It requires designing environments where responsibility is shared, curiosity is protected, and participation carries real weight. Trust means involving students in shaping their learning now, not waiting until they are older or judged "ready."

TOWARD LEARNER-LED FUTURES

If we want democratic societies, we need democratic schools. If we want creative thinkers, we must stop punishing curiosity. And if we want inclusive systems, we must include students in how those systems are governed. Students must be afforded agency, with rights and responsibilities that are real.

This requires a redesign of mainstream education. It means giving up control that was never fairly held and returning to respect and trust as first principles. Students are already thinking, choosing, becoming. Whether we recognize that kids are people, too, will determine whether education becomes a practice of liberation or another instrument of control.

4

Schools must be havens of uncommon safety and extraordinary respect

Education is failing a basic task: preparing people to be human in a complex, interconnected world. Schools claim to shape the leaders, innovators, and citizens of tomorrow, yet many still rely on models that prize compliance over curiosity, standardization over self-awareness, and competition over collaboration. If schools do not become havens of uncommon safety and extraordinary respect, they will keep producing people who can memorize formulas but cannot resolve conflict, who can follow instructions but struggle to form authentic relationships, and who are trained for tests but unprepared for life.

It is not enough to teach information. Schools must cultivate the capacity to navigate human relationships with empathy, self-awareness, and resilience. Without that foundation, learning stays shallow, detached, and hard to use in the world. This is why *Manifesto 25* emphasizes social-emotional and relational intelligence. The fourth point was suggested by Alex Wiedemann, a co-initiator of a democratic learning initiative in Germany.

From *Manifesto 25*:
> ***Schools must be havens of uncommon safety and extraordinary respect.*** *Social-emotional and relational intelligence must be at the core, beyond test scores and rigid academics, fostering empathy, self-awareness, and constructive conflict resolution. The opportunity to be vulnerable in a*

*safe space allows for genuine, authentic connections with others and oneself.
In this way, schools establish the interpersonal foundation learners need to
navigate diverse perspectives and thrive in an interconnected world. These
intelligences are not optional; they are the cornerstone of personal growth
and collective progress.*

Most schools still define success in narrow academic terms, treating emotional
intelligence as a nice extra rather than a necessity. But the ability to communicate, empathize, and resolve conflict is not extracurricular. It is the foundation
for learning and collaboration. A student who excels in calculus but cannot
handle feedback or work through disagreement will struggle in any workplace
or community. A gifted writer who never has space to explore vulnerability may
never develop the confidence to take creative risks (Durlak *et al.*, 2011; Jones *et
al.*, 2017; OECD, 2021).

True intellectual growth demands more than access to content. It
requires the courage to question, to fail, and to speak honestly in difficult
conversations. A classroom built on uncommon safety and extraordinary respect
does not protect students from challenge. It equips them to face it. When learners
trust that their ideas will be met with curiosity rather than ridicule, they take
intellectual risks. They move beyond memorization into inquiry. They argue
with care. They develop the resilience needed for complexity. Without that
foundation, learning becomes performance instead of discovery.

A school that prioritizes relational intelligence does not tolerate
disrespect, whether it shows up as bullying, systemic inequity, or dismissive
responses to student concerns. It builds structures for dialogue. It treats conflict
as a moment for learning, not a problem to be hidden or crushed. Respect is not
manners. It is a commitment to take other people's experiences seriously.

Consider the difference between a classroom where students fear
embarrassment and one where they feel safe enough to take risks. In the first,
participation is cautious, discussion stays shallow, and learning becomes
transactional. In the second, students push their thinking further, debate ideas
openly, and build the capacity to recover from setbacks. The same contrast
appears in discipline. A school that relies only on punishment teaches compliance, not resolution. A school that guides students through understanding harm,

acknowledging impact, and repairing relationships teaches skills they will use for life.

One practical pathway is to *embed restorative justice into daily school life*. Instead of defaulting to suspensions or detentions, schools can create facilitated spaces where students address conflicts, repair harm, and rebuild trust. When conflict arises, a restorative circle can bring those involved together to speak from their perspectives, listen without interruption, and work toward meaningful resolution. This approach can reduce repeat conflict while teaching empathy and accountability in real time (Darling-Hammond *et al.*, 2020; Gregory *et al.*, 2016).

Another pathway is to *teach vulnerability through reflective learning spaces*. In a culture that rewards performance over process, students learn to hide uncertainty and avoid admitting what they do not know. Schools can counter this by building reflective practices into the curriculum: journaling, dialogue circles, and personal storytelling. A literature class might begin the week with short reflections on how a novel's themes connect to students' lives. A science class might ask students to document failures as evidence of learning, treating mistakes as part of discovery. These small, consistent practices create a culture where honesty is safe and growth becomes visible.

A deeper shift comes from *embracing democratic education*, where students have real voice in shaping their learning environment. This means moving beyond token "student councils" that plan events and involving students in decisions that shape daily life. Schools committed to democratic practice hold regular assemblies where students and staff discuss rules, learning priorities, and community concerns. Some involve students in hiring committees for new teachers, recognizing that those most affected by these choices deserve a real say. When students are treated as contributors rather than recipients, respect becomes mutual, and the school becomes practice for civic life (Fielding & Moss, 2011; Mitra, 2018).

None of this is easy. It requires schools to challenge long-held assumptions about authority, discipline, and who gets to decide. But the payoff is real. Schools that center social-emotional and relational intelligence do not only produce stronger students. They produce stronger thinkers, collaborators, and citizens, people equipped to live with others, lead with integrity, and build a more just and humane society.

Social-emotional and relational intelligence are neither optional nor secondary to academic achievement. They are what make learning usable, relationships possible, and lives meaningful. Schools and learning communities must treat this responsibility not as an elective, but as the core of what education is for.

5
Authentic learning comes from freedom, not from being pushed into a pre-determined path

For too long, education has been structured around control. Students are placed on predetermined paths, told what to learn, when to learn it, and how success will be measured. The result is compliance mistaken for education. Schools reward those who follow instructions and penalize those who deviate, confusing obedience with mastery. Curiosity, the engine of real learning, is suppressed. Intrinsic motivation erodes. Learning becomes a passive act, something done to students rather than something they pursue with agency and purpose.

This is a failure of design, not ability. Humans are natural learners. Given room to explore, question, and experiment, people seek knowledge because they want to understand. But when education becomes a chain of tasks to complete instead of a process of discovery, even the most inquisitive minds disengage. To repair this, we must move beyond rigid top-down models that cast teachers as gatekeepers and students as empty vessels. We need flat, collaborative learning that values peer teaching and peer learning, shared responsibility, and the freedom to learn at a pace that fits the learner (Reeve, 2012; Mitra, 2018).

THE THRILL OF JUMPING OFF A CLIFF BY DECIDING TO DO SO YOURSELF IS A HIGH YOU WILL NEVER HAVE IF SOMEONE ELSE PUSHES YOU OFF OF IT.

This point in *Manifesto 25* was inspired by a decade-old conversation with Marcel Kampman, who emphasized the importance of being provided agency to try new things on our own volition:

From *Manifesto 25*:

> ***Authentic learning comes from freedom, not from being pushed into a predetermined path.*** *The traditional top-down, teacher-student model suppresses curiosity and erodes intrinsic motivation, reducing learning to compliance exercises. Instead, we must adopt flat, collaborative approaches that value peer learning, peer teaching, and distributed responsibility. Educators must create environments where students can decide when and how to take their leaps, knowing that failure is not an endpoint but a natural step in the learning process. Failing is a natural part of learning where we can always try again. In a flat learning environment, the teacher's role is to help make sure the learner makes a well-balanced decision. Failing is part of the path of learning, but the creation of failures is not.*

Authentic learning comes from freedom, not from being pushed into a predetermined path. The traditional top-down, teacher-student model suppresses curiosity and erodes intrinsic motivation, reducing learning to compliance exercises. Instead, we must adopt flat, collaborative approaches that value peer learning, peer teaching, and distributed responsibility. Educators must create environments where students can decide when and how to take their leaps, knowing that failure is not an endpoint but a natural step in the learning process. Failing is a natural part of learning where we can always try again. In a *flat* learning environment, the teacher's role is to help make sure the learner makes a well-balanced decision. Failure belongs to the path of learning; it should emerge from exploration, not be engineered into the system.

Authentic learning begins when students take ownership of their education. This does not mean abandoning structure or leaving students to fend for themselves. It means building environments where learners can make real decisions about their learning: when to push forward, when to ask for guidance, and when to pause and reassess. It means allowing failure without shame, recognizing that failure is not a dead end but a necessary, even productive, part of learning. In a flat learning environment, educators do not dictate the terms of success. They facilitate. They help learners make well-balanced decisions. They guide without coercion.

Education often treats failure as something to avoid, a mark of personal inadequacy rather than a normal part of growth. That mindset harms learners. Failing is not the problem. Our response to it is. In a learner-driven environment, failure is information, a signal to reflect and recalibrate, not a verdict on ability. This does not mean manufacturing failure or setting students up to lose. There is a difference between creating room for risk and designing traps. The goal is a space where mistakes function as steps forward, not punishments imposed by the system (Kapur, 2016; Dweck, 2006).

Some of the deepest learning happens outside classrooms, in places where curiosity leads, and often in informal contexts (Rogoff, 2003). A child learns to ride a bike not because it is assigned, but because they want to. They try. They wobble. They fall. They adjust. Motivation comes from within, and learning sticks because it serves a goal the learner chose. The same pattern holds for learning a language, building a scientific hypothesis, or making art. The more agency learners have, the more meaningful learning becomes.

This is common sense, not radical change. Implementing it, however, requires rethinking assumptions about power and control in education. If we believe learning matters, we must stop forcing students down rigid paths and start building systems that trust them to take their own leaps. Education should not be about meeting predetermined benchmarks. It should create the conditions in which learners can flourish on their own terms.

Education beyond the old models

FRAMING

Education faces a paradox. The future is here, but schools remain rooted in past models. Across the world, small and scattered innovations have shown glimpses of what is possible, yet mainstream education lags behind, clinging to structures designed for another era. We cannot expect 1.0 schools to meet the needs of learners who live in 3.0, 4.0, or 5.0 worlds. If we want education to prepare people to create meaningful futures, we must reframe its purpose and design.

This begins with recognizing that learners are not products of the system but people with voices, rights, and agency. Children and young adults must be seen as full human beings who deserve a say in how they learn and in how their schools are governed. Their participation is not a privilege; it is a matter of rights and inclusion.

For schools to honor this, they must be places of safety and respect, where relational intelligence is cultivated with as much seriousness as academic knowledge. Learners need spaces where they can be vulnerable, understood, and supported, not judged by narrow measures of performance. These conditions enable authentic growth and prepare them to thrive in diverse, interconnected communities.

But safety and respect alone are not enough. Learning must be freed from the predetermined tracks that reduce it to compliance. Genuine education emerges when students have the freedom to pursue their own directions, supported by educators who act as guides, collaborators, and colearners. In these environments, mistakes are not punishments but steppingstones toward deeperunderstanding.

To move forward, education must stop copying the past and instead embrace futures that already exist in fragments. We must learn from these living experiments, connect them, and scale them. The choice before us is whether to cling to obsolete models or to co-create education that empowers learners as full participants in shaping the future.

PROMPTS FOR REFLECTION

1. **System vs. self.** When did you realize that schooling was shaping you to serve the system rather than preparing you for your own future? What did you lose (or gain) in that moment?
2. **Entrenched routines.** Which practices in your school, university, or workplace feel like relics from another century? Why do they persist, and who benefits from keeping them alive?
3. **Safety vs. compliance.** Have you ever felt silenced, shamed, or unsafe in a learning space? What structures or cultures created that environment, and what would it take to dismantle them?
4. **Learners as people.** If every student's rights and agency were taken seriously, what rules, rituals, or power structures would have to disappear tomorrow?
5. **Freedom to fail.** Where in your current learning or work do you feel genuinely free to take risks, fail, and try again? Where are you punished for it instead?

Try this

Pull out a sheet of paper or use the notes pages that follow. Map one week of your learning or work life. Where have you seen or experienced moments of genuine freedom, where curiosity, experimentation, or even failure became the path to deeper learning?

notes

Notes

Notes

Notes

6

Learning together, teaching together

THE TROUBLE WITH SEPARATING LEARNERS BY AGE SILOS

Most schools group students strictly by age, moving them year by year through parallel cohorts. This structure simplifies scheduling and curriculum delivery, but it also narrows the social and cognitive range of experience available to learners. Children spend most of their day with peers at the same developmental stage, while adults, parents, elders, neighbors, are pushed to the margins of formal learning. Education becomes something *done* to children, not *with* children or with the communities that surround them.

Age-based grouping in education emerged from industrial-era ideals of efficiency and control, simplifying instruction but narrowing learners' exposure to diverse perspectives. Outside of school, we rarely live, work, or solve problems only with people our age. Yet schools isolate learners from one of the richest educational resources available: each other.

But learning has never truly been age-bound. Across cultures and throughout history, knowledge has been passed down through shared labor, storytelling, imitation, and dialogue between generations. Farmers and blacksmiths taught apprentices; grandparents taught traditions and values; siblings learned by doing together. These organic learning arrangements fostered trust, resilience, and a sense of shared purpose. They also allowed individuals to move fluidly between roles as learners and teachers.

Today, research confirms the value of intergenerational learning. Studies show that older students who mentor younger ones develop empathy, leadership skills, and a deeper understanding of their own knowledge. Younger students gain confidence, personalized support, and inspiration. Adults who engage in learning communities with youth report increased well-being, renewed purpose, and stronger social ties. Children benefit from exposure to diverse life experiences, cultural practices, and problem-solving approaches that no textbook could offer (Newman & Hatton-Yeo, 2008; Kaplan, 2002).

Intergenerational learning is vital for navigating the complexity of modern life. No one generation holds all the answers. Elders bring historical memory and lived wisdom, while younger people offer adaptability and new ideas. When these perspectives are brought together, education shifts from rote instruction to relational learning. This facilitates an exchange of insight, care, and shared problem-solving.

From *Manifesto 25*:

> *Learning together, teaching together. Education thrives when everyone becomes both a teacher and a learner. By breaking free from artificial age silos, schools can evolve into vibrant hubs where children, parents, elders, and community members exchange skills, insights, and creativity as open knowledge and networking ecosystems. Older students mentor younger peers while gaining fresh perspectives, and parents and community leaders bring real-world knowledge, enriched by the curiosity of children. This dynamic, reciprocal process celebrates intergenerational wisdom, strengthens social bonds, and empowers all to shape a meaningful future.*

LEARNING BEYOND AGE SILOS

Outside of school, life is intergenerational. Families, communities, and work-places depend on relationships across ages. Schools should reflect that reality, not deny it. When learners are placed in chronological silos, they lose daily opportunities to learn from the broader human experience.

Breaking this structure requires redesigning schools as *shared ecosystems of knowledge*. Older students become both learners and mentors, modeling growth while developing responsibility. Younger students are not passive recipients but active participants whose questions surface new insight. Educators learn alongside students, modeling intellectual humility and the stance of lifelong learning.

The benefits of dissolving age silos are well established in practice. Peer tutoring programs often show gains for both tutor and tutee in academic growth, communication, and self-confidence. Mixed-age classrooms, common in Montessori and democratic schools, tend to support collaboration, autonomy, and emotional maturity. Community-based learning that includes parents and elders strengthens cultural exchange and civic connection.

When schools welcome people of different ages into learning, they become civic spaces. Learning becomes embedded in relationships. Education gains social depth. People are valued for what they can contribute, not defined by what they lack. The classroom expands, and so does the imagination of what education can be.

EVERYONE A LEARNER, EVERYONE A TEACHER

In a healthy learning ecosystem, roles stay fluid. Children teach. Elders learn. Teachers admit uncertainty. Parents model curiosity. The idea that knowledge flows only one way, from expert to novice, flattens human experience and confuses information transfer with learning. Personal knowledge is constructed continuously. We are all learners and teachers, often at the same time.

Reciprocity requires a shift in mindset. It means taking insight seriously wherever it appears, regardless of age, title, or credentials. A younger student might teach an older one to code. A grandparent might pass on storytelling techniques or gardening wisdom. A local artist might co-create a mural with children, blending technique with imagination. To sustain this culture, schools must design for reciprocal exchange. That means shaping physical, social, and cultural spaces that bring generations together around shared work. Examples already exist in both formal and nonformal settings.

1. Multigenerational learning hubs

Schools can partner with local libraries, community centers, and makerspaces to create hubs where elders and youth engage in joint projects. For example, Whatcom Intergenerational High School in Washington state incorporates regular visits from community elders who help co-lead seminars, fostering critical dialogue across age groups. These hubs offer both formal and informal learning experiences, combining mentorship, storytelling, and collaborative problem-solving.

2. Timebanking and skill-sharing networks

Inspired by community time bank models, schools can implement systems where people offer their expertise in exchange for learning something new. A retired mechanic might teach hands-on physics through bicycle repair; a teenager could tutor digital skills in return. The Intergenerational Learning Center at St. Joseph's Home in Singapore is one such example, where elders and children regularly engage in reciprocal caregiving and storytelling activities.

3. Gardens and outdoor classrooms

Shared cultivation projects offer a powerful setting for learning. In Japan, intergenerational learning gardens, such as Okayama Education for Sustainable Development Project, bring elders and children together to grow vegetables, discuss seasonal changes, and exchange cultural knowledge. These gardens not only deepen understanding of ecological cycles and food systems but also strengthen respect across generations. Research by Wang, Huang, & Lee (2023) supports that such programs foster emotional bonds, improve dietary knowledge, and create collaborative learning experiences across age groups.

4. Co-designed curriculum projects

Students, parents, and community members can collaborate to co-design parts of the curriculum. For example, in some New Zealand schools influenced by Māori pedagogies, whānau (extended family) participate in planning and delivering content tied to cultural history, values, and language (Neha, *et al.*, 2020). This approach centers learning as a collective responsibility and embeds it in place, identity, and belonging.

5. Neighborhood and community networks

Instead of isolating learning in classrooms, schools can adopt a networked approach, encouraging students to conduct oral histories, map neighborhood assets, or work with civic leaders on local challenges. Intergenerational projects grounded in local context make learning tangible and participatory. One example is the Shibuya University Network, which facilitates free, community-interest classes for and by people from all walks of life.

Across these strategies, the goal is to move beyond token involvement and toward genuine collaboration. Intergenerational learning becomes transformative when all participants feel valued, responsible, and capable of contributing. It is not about transferring static knowledge from old to young, but about forming living relationships that adapt and grow.

In designing for this kind of education, we must ask: *Who is included in the learning process? Whose knowledge counts? How can we create ecosystems where everyone, regardless of age, has a role to play in shaping what we know and how we live together?* By empowering everyone to teach and learn, education becomes less about status and more about participation. It becomes less about control and more about contribution.

STRATEGIES FOR CULTIVATING INTERGENERATIONAL LEARNING

To move from aspiration to reality, intergenerational learning must be supported through structures that promote trust, collaboration, and shared responsibility. Below are five practical strategies, each grounded in real-world models that schools and communities can adopt to create vibrant, reciprocal learning ecosystems.

1. Create shared learning spaces

Design welcoming environments where learners of all ages collaborate on shared projects. These might include multi-use classrooms, makerspaces, public libraries, or outdoor learning hubs that invite informal gathering and exploration. Successful shared learning spaces depend on flexible infrastructure that accommodates a wide range of physical, sensory, and social needs. Designs must prioritize comfort, accessibility, and openness to allow people of all ages to move, rest, and interact comfortably. Just as important is a shared governance model that invites all participants, including children and elders, to help define how the space is used and maintained. These co-created norms foster trust, accountability, and a sense of belonging.

2. Foster peer mentorship across ages

Build routines that pair older students with younger ones for academic help, creative projects, or personal storytelling. Older mentors gain leadership skills, while younger students receive encouragement and personalized guidance. Mentorship programs require intentional scheduling:dedicated time within the school day when students can build trust across age groups. Older students benefit from basic training on how to support their younger peers, as well as opportunities to reflect on the experience and their growth as mentors. These programs thrive when schools recognize mentorship not as an extracurricular add-on, but as a core learning activity, validating the time and attention it takes to build strong relationships.

3. Invite community members to co-teach

Create regular opportunities for parents, elders, artisans, and local workers to share their skills and stories in the classroom alongside formal educators. For co-teaching to succeed, school leadership must be open to redefining who is a "teacher." This includes revisiting policies around classroom access, safety, and instructional design. Curriculum frameworks should include space for community-based knowledge and allow for nonlinear, experience-driven approaches to learning. Crucially, building and maintaining trust with community partners requires sustained outreach, listening, and responsiveness, particularly with groups who have historically been excluded from schools.

4. Embed learning in real community projects

Shift classrooms into neighborhoods. Let intergenerational teams work on local challenges such as ecological restoration, food justice, or oral history. Schools must build long-term relationships with community organizations, civic leaders, and families to co-design learning projects that are relevant, respectful, and rooted in place. This requires partnership agreements that define roles, expectations, and mutual benefits. Assessment models also need to evolve, valuing process, collaboration, and impact over narrow content delivery. Finally, these projects demand time. Longer cycles of engagement that allow trust to form, challenges to emerge, and solutions to evolve.

5. Honor diverse literacies and ways of knowing

Treat oral traditions, embodied practice, and lived experience as valid forms of knowledge beyond written text or standardized content. Educators must be supported in developing culturally sustaining pedagogies that embrace multiple literacies such as storytelling, movement, craft, or digital creation. This involves both professional learning and structural flexibility to allow different modes of assessment, expression, and feedback. Classrooms must also become dialogic spaces, where knowledge is built through conversation, reflection, and performance rather than extracted through tests or rigid assignments.

Intergenerational learning reflects how humans have learned for most of history. When schools open to the wider world and invite everyone to teach and learn, education regains its social purpose. It becomes a living system of reciprocity rooted in trust, connection, and shared growth.

By welcoming diverse voices, softening age boundaries, and valuing everyday wisdom, we build not only more inclusive classrooms, but stronger communities. Learning expands when we learn with and from one another across generations, backgrounds, and lived experience. Education thrives when it stops drawing lines between us and starts building the bridges we all need.

7
No more boxes: Learning in ecosystems

Learning 'outside of the box' is cliché.
Forget the box!

Most formal education divides life into compartments. Math at 10 a.m. Science after lunch. Curiosity, if time allows. The structure is tidy and predictable. Real learning is neither. It is messy: contextual, relational, and often spontaneous. Despite decades of reform, most schools still rely on fragmentation. Subjects remain isolated. Schedules stay rigid. Learners are grouped into simple cohorts and separated from the complexity of the world they inhabit.

From *Manifesto 25*:

> ***Learning occurs in ecosystems, not boxes.*** *Rigid schedules and siloed classrooms reduce education to a transactional process, ignoring its lifelong, interwoven nature. Formal schooling should be one strand in a wider tapestry of experiences that involves family, community, workplaces, and digital networks. By blending these contexts, we erase boundaries between formal and informal learning, allowing knowledge and skills to circulate freely. In such environments, students learn to adapt to various roles, work across generations, and embrace insights from unexpected sources. Freed from the confines of boxes, education fuels curiosity and self-confidence, preparing learners to flourish in an ever-evolving world.*

RETHINKING WHERE, AND HOW, LEARNING HAPPENS

Learning does not begin or end in classrooms during industrial work hours. Families, community centers, libraries, maker spaces, online forums, and workplaces all shape what people know and how they grow. These spaces are vital parts of how we learn (Ito, 2013; Barron, 2006).

Consider Sofia, a 14-year-old in Buenos Aires. At school, she struggles with traditional writing assignments. But outside class, she runs a food review blog with her older cousin, writing, editing, and promoting posts on Instagram and TikTok. She translates posts to engage a wider audience and partners with local cafés to feature and promote their work. None of this appears in her school record. However, she is developing communication skills, digital literacy, and entrepreneurial thinking, each skills the curriculum claims to value.

When schools ignore learning beyond their walls, they disconnect students from their own lives. Most systems still treat community knowledge as enrichment rather than essential learning. Recognizing what learners like Sofia already do would connect the dots: linking informal experience to academic goals and translating problem-solving into recognized achievements.

This shift prompts us to design for relevance without lowering standards. Schools can build flexible schedules to allow time for internships, fieldwork, or community service. They can offer credit for real-world projects and create tools for students to track and reflect on learning across contexts. Educators become guides who help learners build bridges between home, school, and world, not gatekeepers of where learning starts and stops. In a healthy, functioning ecosystem, schools connect knowledge more than they deliver information (Wenger, 1998; Brown & Duguid, 2000). This implies *attending to new knowledge creation* rather than trying to managing it.

FROM TRANSACTION TO CIRCULATION

Despite decades of reform, many schools continue to function like delivery systems: knowledge is packaged, delivered, and measured through controlled processes. This model treats learning as an isolated transaction, missing how real growth circulates across relationships, places, and experiences. Despite calls for reform, schooling still operates like a delivery system: teachers hand down content, students are expected to absorb it, and tests are used to validate the exchange. This transactional model reinforces separation between disciplines, between learners and their communities, and between education and lived experience (Biesta, 2013; Freire, 1970). It overlooks how real learning happens: across relationships, through curiosity, and in response to the world.

An ecosystem model works differently. Knowledge moves. It grows through interaction, conversation, trial and error. It is shared across communities and adapted through lived experience. In contrast, ecosystem learning grows through interaction, experimentation, and reflection. Knowledge is shared, remixed, and reinterpreted across relationships and settings, becoming something learners contribute to in addition to consumption.

It is important to understand this shift. The challenges young people (or any of us) face do not fall neatly into categories. Addressing climate collapse, food security, or purposive use of AI requires integrating ideas from many fields and perspectives. Success in these spaces depends on the ability to collaborate with people who think differently, ask better questions, and find connections across domains.

When learning is designed for circulation, schools become nodes in a larger network of shared knowledge and mutual learning, a role that extends beyond content delivery. Teachers organize conditions for inquiry. Learners contribute knowledge, draw from their communities, and test ideas through action. A science teacher may collaborate with a local farm. A media project might involve elders sharing oral histories. A math project could map energy use in neighborhood buildings. The learning continues wherever relationships can be formed and questions pursued, non-stop.

This approach changes the role of the school in society. Rather than gatekeeping knowledge, schools create flow. They connect people, ideas, and experiences that might otherwise remain siloed. They make learning visible and relevant across the contexts where it already happens. In doing so, they help learners develop the skills, empathy, and agility needed to meet the complexity of the present and shape what comes next.

DESIGNING FOR ECOSYSTEMS

Moving toward an ecosystem approach requires more than expanding where learning happens. It calls for a new way of thinking about how learning is structured, supported, and recognized. Schools must shift from acting as the central authority to becoming active participants in a broader network.

1. Flexible pathways

Learners follow many routes to knowledge. Personalized learning plans should account for learning that happens outside of school walls (e.g., through internships, caregiving, online communities, artistic practice, activism, and part-time work). These experiences provide legitimate, often more durable, sources of growth.

2. Networked partnerships

No single institution can meet the needs of today's learners. Schools must work closely with libraries, museums, local businesses, community organizations, and cultural centers. These partners help build relevant, applied learning opportunities. A design student might work with an urban planning office. A group studying migration could collaborate with a local refugee support group.

3. Intergenerational learning spaces

Most school environments group learners by age. In contrast, learning ecosystems allow learners to engage with people of different generations. A teenager might learn carpentry from a neighbor, mentor a younger student in robotics, or co-host a podcast with a grandparent. These interactions foster empathy, resilience, and the ability to navigate different perspectives.

4. Open recognition systems

Learners need ways to document what they know and what they can do, especially when their learning does not come from traditional classrooms. Portfolios, digital badges, public exhibitions, and references from community members can offer meaningful evidence of growth. Recognition becomes more about relationships and impact than about test scores.

5. Community-based inquiry

Learning becomes more powerful when rooted in place. Projects that respond to local challenges (such as food access, water quality, or community storytelling) help learners build a sense of purpose while developing skills. These local projects often connect to larger questions, giving learners insight into global patterns through personal engagement.

Schools do not disappear in this design; They evolve. They no longer try to contain learning within narrow structures. Instead, they become hubs in a larger web: curators of opportunity, builders of trust, and partners in a lifelong learning process. The intended outcome is to build education into a lived, participatory experience.

BREAKING FREE FROM BOXES

Education has long relied on boxes. They are easy to manage. Classrooms, periods, and age bands exist to regulate movement and standardize measurement so learners emerge as standardized workers. Learning does not follow those lines. It moves across places, ideas, and relationships. An ecosystem approach accepts this movement and treats lived experience as a source of depth, not disorder.

These environments are porous. They allow movement between places, ideas, and communities. Learners bring with them experience, insight, and motivation from beyond school walls. Just like Sofia in Buenos Aires, whose online work reveals talents hidden by traditional assignments, many young people already operate in rich learning ecosystems that many adults fail to recognize.

When learning is tied to the real world, people begin to see it differently. A middle school student who helps translate documents at a clinic learns applied literacy and civic responsibility. A high schooler who manages a small business with their family develops financial skills, problem-solving, and collaboration. These moments are valued as "places" where learning happens.

When learners see that their work has meaning (to themselves, to their communities, to the world) they begin to trust that learning is worth the effort. Learning ecosystems invite schools to grow into life.

8

Learning at the intersection of agency and self-efficacy

At the heart of meaningful education is a powerful idea: learners thrive when they are trusted to shape their learning and believe they are capable of success. This fusion of agency (being afforded real choices) and self-efficacy (believing in one's ability to act on those choices) transforms education from routine compliance into purposeful growth.

From *Manifesto 25*:

> *Nirvana is found in the fusion of agency with self-efficacy.*
> *When learners and educators achieve both agency (the freedom to shape their paths) and self-efficacy (the belief that they can succeed) education transcends traditional goals and reaches its ultimate purpose: empowering individuals to lead fulfilling, impactful lives. Schools should actively cultivate this balance by blending choice-driven learning with consistent opportunities for learners to build and demonstrate competence. This fusion prepares students for the future by enabling the inspiration and vision necessary to create it.*

Agency without self-efficacy leads to aimless drift. A learner with options but lacking skills or confidence may disengage. Self-efficacy without agency becomes obedience. Learners follow others' plans but don't lead their own. Empowerment emerges when people are free and able to make meaningful decisions, reflect on progress, and adapt with purpose.

Too often, schools fall short on both. What is presented as "alternatives" or "choices" becomes a set of false selections, based on shallow decisions such as electives, paint colors, or seating arrangements, while competence is measured through high-stakes tests. Learners navigate a system that respects neither autonomy nor confidence. To change this, learning environments must support both freedom and growth. This means co-designing learning goals, offering diverse ways to show understanding, and making space for iteration, failure, and reflection. Learners who reflect on progress and understand that growth is within their control take initiative, persist, and think creatively about the future.

THE MIND NEEDS BOTH AGENCY AND SELF-EFFICACY

Neuroscience and psychology confirm what many educators know: learning flourishes when people feel both autonomous and capable. Agency, the sense of control over actions, is key to motivation. When learners make real choices, the brain releases dopamine, which fuels curiosity and engagement. According to self-determination theory (Deci & Ryan, 1985), autonomy improves performance, creativity, and perseverance. Self-efficacy, the belief in one's ability to succeed, is equally important. Psychologist Albert Bandura (1997) found that self-efficacy predicts effort, how learners handle setbacks, and whether they persist. Belief in ability leads to resilience and growth.

Cognitive science shows that decision-making and goal-setting engage the prefrontal cortex, strengthening planning, self-regulation, and adaptability. When learners practice agency and experience progress, they develop habits of mind that support lifelong learning. The fusion of agency and self-efficacy supports motivation, mental health, and flexible thinking. It is essential for deep, meaningful learning.

A central theme in *Manifesto 25* is that mainstream education is built on outdated assumptions about motivation and learning, often prioritizing obedience over curiosity. When schools restrict agency and self-efficacy, they suppress genuine learning. Environments that support real growth do both: they offer meaningful choices and reinforce the belief that individuals can act on them. This dual focus, choice and confidence, helps people navigate uncertainty with clarity, resilience, and purpose.

DESIGNING FOR THE FUSION OF AGENCY AND SELF-EFFICACY

Fusing agency and self-efficacy requires actions that go beyond surface-level change. It means rethinking how learning is structured and supported. Here are five design principles that help make this possible:

1. Curriculum that fosters ownership and purpose

Invite learners into curriculum design, where relevance fuels motivation, and where motivation deepens learning. Build flexibility into what and how people learn without losing depth. Frame learning around open-ended, interdisciplinary problems:

- *How can we make our campus more sustainable?*
- *Who gets remembered in history, and why?*

2. Assessment that builds confidence instead of compliance

Self-efficacy grows through real progress. Use transparent, varied, and formative assessment. Portfolios, peer feedback, public presentations, and goal-setting help learners view learning as growth.

3. Structures that support autonomy without abandoning learners

Agency needs support. Weekly planning, check-ins, reflection journals, and advisory periods help learners manage complexity. These routines support autonomy.

4. A culture of trust, high expectations, and belonging

Self-efficacy grows in safe environments. Build a culture of shared norms, mutual respect, and recognition. When learners know their voice matters, they believe they can make a difference.

5. Educators need agency and self-efficacy, too

Educators are learning designers, not content deliverers. They ask questions, offer feedback, and learn with others. This requires time, trust, and autonomy. A system that denies agency to educators cannot build it in learners.

IN PRACTICE...

When we look at learning environments that support both agency and self-efficacy, we do not find disorder. We find focus, energy, and purpose. These spaces are structured with intention. They give learners freedom, along with the tools to use it well. Boundaries are clear, but they exist to support experimentation and growth. Learners are doing work that is important to them, guided by expectations they help define with peers and educators.

At High Tech High in the United States, learners co-design projects with teachers, present their ideas, revise their work, and share it publicly. In Lumiar Schools in Brazil, they shape their education by selecting thematic challenges. Progress is tracked through portfolios and regular conversations, not test scores. In Finland, learners take part in class meetings where they help decide on classroom norms, learning goals, and priorities.

Of course, these are not isolated examples and we can see bits of agency and self-efficacy fused together in various environments. However, these examples show how schools can be built differently. With the right structures, learners are treated as thoughtful, capable people. They are given space to grow, but also asked to take responsibility for that growth. When this balance is in place, school becomes a place of purpose, not routine.

Changing how schools work means questioning old habits. It means moving past the idea that education is about control. As stated in the manifesto, the purpose of education is not to make people fit into the world as it is, but to help them imagine how it could be—*and help them bring it to life*. Agency and self-efficacy should not be treated as something that is separate from a curriculum. They are what make this kind of learning possible.

When people *know* they have real choices, and believe they can make a difference, they stop waiting for the future. They begin to shape it. Schools that support this mindset prepare learners to lead the future.

9
Teachers at the crossroads

We ask teachers to prepare students for an unpredictable, AI-infused, climate-volatile world. Yet we treat those same educators as if their job is to execute instructions, not co-create solutions.

This what happens in a system designed to replicate itself. But a good education does not happen without interpretation. It is a deeply contextual, improvisational, and relational act. If we want young people to learn how to collaborate, adapt, and think critically, then their teachers must be empowered to model those capacities. Teaching must be understood as intellectual work that is complex, creative, and consequential.

From *Manifesto 25*:

> ***Educators are creators, collaborators, and innovators, not cogs in a machine.*** *Reducing them to implementers of legacy methods undermines both learners and the future of education. To address the demands of a dynamic, interconnected world, educators must be valued as individuals with unique needs, aspirations, and creative potential. Transforming education means enabling educators as co-creators, equipping them with trust, tools, and resources to drive innovation. Recognizing educators as professionals and partners fosters thriving learning environments where both teachers and students flourish, inspiring curiosity, adaptability, and resilience.*

LIFE IN THE MACHINE

Over the past four decades, waves of neoliberal reform have recast teachers as implementers of external mandates (that is, *deliverers* of content rather than *designers*). In the name of "accountability," policymakers have introduced scripted curricula, high-stakes testing, and performance management tools designed to measure fidelity, not imagination. As Stephen Ball (2003) observes, this regime of managerialism transforms educators into policy delivery mechanisms, alienated from their own work. Michael Apple (2004) goes further, arguing that this technocratic turn strips teachers of professional autonomy and serves a political agenda of depoliticized, market-aligned schooling.

The symptoms are everywhere:

- **Curriculum narrowing** that rewards testable content over deep learning.
- **Real-time surveillance** via learning management systems and AI tools that quantify every click and keystroke.
- **Evaluation frameworks** that reduce complex pedagogical work to rubrics and checklists.
- **Burnout and attrition** driven by demoralization and from the erosion of purpose (Santoro, 2011).

This is bad for learning. When educators are denied space to exercise professional judgment, creativity disappears from the classroom. Risk-taking evaporates. Students learn to perform, not to inquire. The result? A profession in crisis. A pipeline problem not because people don't want to teach, but because they no longer recognize the work as professional. The joy of teaching (i.e., designing experiences, supporting discovery, responding to the needs of real learners) is slowly being automated, outsourced, or erased.

Yet research consistently shows that teacher agency is as critically important for educator wellbeing as it is for student outcomes (Bandura 1997; Deci & Ryan, 1985). Teachers who feel trusted, valued, and empowered are more likely to innovate, connect meaningfully with students, and stay in the profession. *Agency* is critical to both the construction of effective learning environments and the professional identity of educators.

We cannot build adaptive, equitable education systems on a foundation of teacher compliance. We need educators who can think, question, and create. But to get there, we must first identify (and dismantle) the systems that have constrained them.

EDUCATORS AS DESIGNERS

If education is to remain adaptive and future-focused, we must stop treating teachers like factory workers. Teaching centers on designing experiences and shaping environments where inquiry thrives, knowledge evolves, and learners take intellectual risks.

Design work goes far beyond curriculum delivery. It requires interpretation, creativity, and responsiveness to context. Teachers make constant decisions about framing questions, pressing for precision, or pausing for care. These are knowledge-based judgments, not tasks to be checked off.

Shifting the paradigm from delivery to design requires recognizing teachers as *knowledge workers*, not as cogs in a machine or compliance officers. As Pantić and Florian (2015) argue, teacher agency is a core driver of meaningful innovation. When educators are empowered to co-create curriculum, adapt pedagogy, and invent new learning ecologies, students receive a much richer experience.

Consider not the usual examples of project-based learning or inquiry units, but the boundary-pushers:

- **Underground curriculum hacking**, where educators subvert prescribed content to include banned books, local histories, or queer epistemologies.
- **Speculative education design**, where educators collaborate with students to imagine future schools, rethinking everything from schedules to assessments to the role of AI.
- **Teaching as social practice**, where classrooms become organizing hubs, designing campaigns, building solidarity, or prototyping mutual aid structures.

This work is grounded in purpose and appears across contexts. From Nairobi to Naples, educators redesign their roles not because systems invite them to, but *because they must*. Networks such as Rethinking Schools, the Human Restoration Project, and teacher-activist collectives in underserved communities model a counter-professionalism that is reflective, insurgent, and creative.

But innovation without infrastructure collapses. To support educators as designers, systems must shift from surveillance to support.

INNOVATION REQUIRES TRUST AND INFRASTRUCTURE

Innovation in education begins with trust.

When policymakers call for "transformation," they often focus on visible, easy to manage tools such as digital platforms, new metrics, slick dashboards. They promise to create meaningful, positive changes, but change rarely happens. Authentic transformation happens at the level of relationships, time, and culture. You cannot automate inspiration. And you cannot systematize innovation by stripping educators of the very conditions that make it possible.

At its core, educational innovation requires three components:

- **Professional autonomy**: Teachers need room to interpret, design, and deviate from scripts that don't serve their learners.
- **Collaborative time**: Not for compliance meetings, but for shared inquiry, dreaming, prototyping, and reflection.
- **Cultures of trust**: Where risk-taking is safe, dissent is welcomed, and learning is mutual between teachers, students, leaders, and communities.

Hargreaves and Fullan (2012) argue, innovation flourishes when schools build "professional capital," where expertise, moral purpose, and shared responsibility guide practice. In contrast, when schools are governed by distrust (e.g., measured by high-stakes tests and managed through top-down mandates) teachers retreat. They protect themselves. Creativity narrows. Burnout accelerates. Those who survive are often the best at playing their roles in the machine, but not the best educators. Across the world, we already see what becomes possible when agency expressed as "professional capital" and trust intersect:

- **In Finland**, teachers operate with high autonomy and deep professional respect.
- **In Ontario**, school improvement networks have shown how collaborative professionalism leads to large-scale pedagogical shifts without compliance regimes.
- **In Latin America**, teacher-led design labs (e.g., Outliers School) have redefined curriculum as a living, local, student-informed practice.

Compare this with systems where surveillance substitutes for support. That is, where algorithmic grading replaces teacher judgment and where "scaling up" means cloning, not cultivating. The result? Demoralized professionals, performative innovation, and classrooms that feel more like test prep centers than communities of learning. We must reframe teaching not as implementation, but as inquiry. Not as fidelity to a plan, but as responsiveness to a shifting world.

This reframing has three policy implications:

- **Shift accountability** from test results to reflective, evidence-informed practice.
- **Embed teacher voice** in curriculum development, education research, and system governance.
- **Rethink teacher preparation** as formation of intellectual and imaginative capacities.

And this reframing also has global urgency. As UNESCO's Teacher Task Force (n.d.) and the OECD's indicators of teacher professionalism (OECD, 2016) highlight, supporting teachers as designers and co-creators is necessary for resilient, equitable education systems. Innovation doesn't come from the top. It comes from the ground, when educators have the autonomy, community, and trust to lead.

THE FUTURE NEEDS TEACHER-CREATORS

We cannot build future-ready education systems by treating teachers like cogs in someone else's design. If we want classrooms that cultivate curiosity, adaptability, and collaboration, then educators must be empowered to practice those very capacities themselves.

This means moving beyond surface reforms and rethinking the profession at its core. Teachers are not merely facilitators of content. They are navigators of uncertainty, stewards of human development, catalysts of civic imagination, and designers of new possibilities. When we reduce their role to compliance, we betray the profession and the future.

Education is a complex system shaped by those who enact it daily. If we want that system to evolve, we must shift from managing teachers to enabling them. That means giving them time to think, space to create, trust to lead, and support to grow.

Empowering educators as creators is an expression of realism in a world that demands ingenuity, care, and courage. Innovations, reforms, or AI tools cannot save education without the people who make learning real every day. If teachers are expected to teach creativity, critical thinking, and collaboration, they must be allowed to practice them first.

10

Don't value what we measure; measure what we value

Mainstream education systems are trapped in a damaging fixation on measurement. Worse, they measure the wrong things. Schools track test scores, attendance, and graduation rates as if these numbers define learning. They do not. High-stakes testing does not improve education. It distorts it. Students learn to perform rather than to understand. Teachers rush to cover material instead of cultivating curiosity and creativity. Policymakers treat test results as evidence of progress while ignoring whether students can think critically, solve problems, or apply knowledge in real contexts.

This paradigm is not new. Standardized testing evolved from intelligence testing and industrial-era efficiency models, gaining significant traction with accountability movements Sahlberg (2015) refers to as the Global Education Reform Movement (GERM). The idea was to ensure public resources were used wisely, a seemingly reasonable goal. However, these policies inadvertently narrowed the curriculum and magnified the perceived importance of easily quantifiable outcomes (Au, 2009; Ravitch, 2010).

From *Manifesto 25*:

> *Don't value what we measure; measure what we value. Assessments should empower learners, not instill fear. The obsession with high-stakes testing abets anxiety and reduces education to rote memorization, sidelining critical thinking and problem-solving. The cult of high-stakes testing has become the misguided arbiters of success, spreading a harmful culture of comparison and underperformance anxiety worldwide. This fixation undermines genuine innovation, with promising ideas dismissed due to measurement concerns. Worse, schools produce leaders ill-equipped to interpret data critically. We must eliminate compulsory high-stakes testing and redirect resources toward initiatives that advance authentic learning and meaningful, multidimensional growth.*

THE ENDURING CULT OF HIGH-STAKES TESTING

Assessment should support learning, not induce fear. Instead, the obsession with high-stakes testing abets anxiety and reduces education to rote memorization, sidelining critical thinking and problem-solving (Kohn, 2000). The "cult of high-stakes testing" has become the misguided arbiter of success, spreading a harmful culture of comparison and underperformance anxiety worldwide. This fixation undermines genuine innovation, often dismissing promising ideas due to measurement concerns. Worse, schools produce leaders ill-equipped to interpret data critically, a crucial skill in a complex world.

High-stakes testing does not empower learners; it conditions them. It rewards rapid recall of data and information and penalizes deeper thinking and genuine expressions of knowledge. This turns learning into performance, replacing exploration and growth with anxiety and fear (Bransford, Brown, & Cocking, 2000). Tests primarily measure compliance rather than capability, encouraging students to avoid challenges for fear of failure. The outcome? Graduates adept at navigating standardized exams but who struggle with complex, unstructured problems that demand creativity and adaptability.

This system also deepens inequity. High-stakes tests often reflect and perpetuate existing societal disparities, disproportionately impacting marginalized student populations: those from low-income backgrounds, racial minorities, English language learners, and students with disabilities. Factors like test bias, unequal access to resources, and culturally biased content mean these exams often measure privilege rather than potential, exacerbating social stratification (Darling-Hammond, 2004; Valenzuela, 1999).

The testing industry perpetuates the myth that success can be quantified by a single number. This has profound consequences. Ideas and skills that cannot be easily measured are dismissed or marginalized. Innovation suffers because it does not conform to established metrics. Schools emphasize measurable subjects at the expense of critical thinking, creative expression, and emotional intelligence—qualities essential for navigating future challenges. The outcome is a workforce proficient at following instructions but lacking the capacity to interpret data critically, question assumptions, or propose innovative solutions (see esp. Zhao, 2009).

For teachers, the impact is equally severe. High-stakes testing narrows curricula, reduces teacher autonomy, and fuels stress and burnout. It can de-professionalize educators, reducing their complex role to mere test preparation, discouraging pedagogical risk-taking, and stifling the very innovation needed to adapt to diverse student needs. Meanwhile, the testing industry itself is a lucrative business, with significant financial incentives and political lobbying influencing education policy, further entrenching these problematic practices (Hursh, 2007).

High-stakes testing is a well-intentioned but misguided attempt at accountability. Governments understandably seek clear indicators of success when investing public resources in education. However, standardized test scores offer only the illusion of clarity. They measure only what is easily quantified, not what is meaningful or valuable. Ironically, testing has become a lucrative, multi-billion dollar business paid for and by governments.

True accountability should not focus on numbers alone but on whether students develop the skills and mindsets needed to thrive beyond school. Education policies must evolve beyond simplistic metrics and toward comprehensive systems that recognize and reward the complexity of authentic learning. This doesn't mean abandoning assessment entirely; it means creating assessments aligned with genuine learning. Schools should assess students' capacity to analyze, synthesize, and apply knowledge.

PATHWAYS TO AUTHENTIC ASSESSMENT

Portfolios, collected over time, illustrate genuine growth by highlighting students' evolving understanding and skills. A student's portfolio might include a science project demonstrating the gradual refinement of a hypothesis through experimentation and feedback. In creative writing, drafts and revisions document how students develop their ideas and expressive abilities over time. Similarly, portfolios in subjects such as mathematics or technology might showcase ongoing projects, including challenges overcome, mistakes made, and innovative solutions generated through iterative problem-solving. These examples reveal deeper layers of learning, creativity, and innovation, elements of personal knowledge development which traditional tests cannot capture. Detailed narrative feedback from teachers provides constructive guidance that numeric scores cannot match.

Effective assessments must support learning rather than merely sorting and ranking students. Assessments should help students grow, providing insights into their strengths and areas for improvement. Peer reviews, collaborative projects, and self-reflective practices encourage ongoing engagement with content and continuous development. Education must move beyond numeric scores to foster active, reflective, and meaningful learning experiences.

Achieving this transformation requires prioritizing human development over mere compliance. Governments must redefine accountability to ensure schools cultivate lifelong learners rather than enforcing rigid benchmarks. Resources currently dedicated to testing and compliance should be redirected to develop assessment methods that capture the complexity and depth of human intelligence (Linn, 2000; National Research Council, 1999).

Decades of research and critique have made these conclusions clear. Yet the system remains largely unchanged. Policies are renamed, but reliance on standardized metrics persists. The literature cited here remains relevant because the problem remains unresolved. The continuity of this failure reflects a sustained unwillingness to prioritize authentic learning over flawed measures that are easy to administer and defend.

Education must measure what truly matters to thrive in the modern world: critical thinking, collaborative skills, creativity, and the capacity to contribute meaningfully to society. Only then can assessment be tooled to empower students and reflect authentic learning.

11
Bad use of technology is a symptom, not the problem

When technology appears to fail in education, we're quick to blame the tools: "The platform is outdated," "The software doesn't work," or "Students are distracted by their devices." Yet, these failures aren't the root cause; they're symptoms of a deeper dysfunction in how we fundamentally approach learning. This is an old problem we've long understood but have done little to address, with educational systems stubbornly clinging to outdated models despite decades of mounting evidence and critique.

From *Manifesto 25*:

> ***Bad use of technology is a symptom, not the problem.*** *Technology is not a solution by itself, but when used thoughtfully, it can unlock new ways of learning and creating. We must move beyond old practices and truly harness technology as a tool for transformation, rather than obsessing over the latest tools while neglecting their potential to drive change. Swapping blackboards for smartboards or books for tablets while clinging to old teaching methods is like building a nuclear plant to power a horse cart: wasteful and ineffective. Yet, nothing has changed, and we still focus tremendous resources on these tools and squander our opportunities to exploit their potential to transform what we learn and how we do it. By recreating practices of the past with technologies, schools focus more on managing hardware and software rather than developing students' mindware and the purposive use of these tools.*

A simple analogy clarifies this point: a hammer, a basic form of technology, can be used to construct or to demolish. Its impact depends entirely on how it is wielded. This same principle must be applied to technology in education.

The core issue is structural. Most education systems are still designed for efficiency and control, shaped by industrial-era priorities that no longer match a fast-changing, uncertain world. Knowledge delivery dominates. Success is measured by compliance rather than insight, creativity, or judgment. When new technologies enter this environment, they are absorbed into the existing logic. They reinforce the old model instead of challenging it (Watters, 2021; Cuban, 2018).

As a result, digital tools become glorified textbooks. Students consume rather than create. Artificial intelligence is reduced to automating grading or administrative work instead of expanding human capability. Learning management systems organize content delivery but rarely support deep engagement or collaborative knowledge building. Technology does not transform learning. It makes traditional practices faster and more scalable (Luckin, 2018). The predictable result is frustration, disengagement, and resistance. Not because the tools fail, but because the system cannot use them well.

Teachers, too, are often left without the support, training, or autonomy to truly innovate. They are told to integrate technology but are rarely given the freedom to rethink their roles as facilitators of learning rather than content deliverers. Meanwhile, students, unable to escape this world of rapid change and radical transformation, find themselves constrained by structures that demand passive absorption rather than participation and active knowledge creation (Ertmer & Ottenbreit-Leftwich, 2010; Tondeur *et al.*, 2012).

Therefore, if technology appears to be failing in education, the solution is not to simply inject more tools into the existing framework. A profound redesign of the learning experience from the ground up is imperative. This necessitates a shift beyond the archaic notion that education is solely about knowledge transfer. Instead, it requires a refocused commitment to creating environments where students learn how to navigate complexity, solve novel problems, and actively shape their own futures. Technology, in this paradigm, should unequivocally amplify human potential, not replace it.

This transformation demands a rethinking of the very architecture of learning. Schools and institutions must evolve from systems of rigid control to dynamic platforms for exploration and co-creation. Learners should be granted genuine agency in how, when, and where they learn. Teachers, in turn, must be empowered to act as visionary designers of knowledge experiences, moving beyond their traditional role as mere content purveyors. Rather than attempting to automate education, we should be leveraging technology to support more adaptive, personalized, and profoundly meaningful learning journeys.

Ultimately, the perceived "bad use of technology" is merely a symptom. The root problem lies in our persistent application of 21st-century tools to a 19th-century education model. Until we courageously address this fundamental disconnect, no amount of "new technology" will fix what is broken; it will only make an outdated system more efficient at producing outdated outcomes.

CAHIER TWO

Beyond measures
and myths

FRAMING

Education is more than the transmission of knowledge within classrooms; it is a living practice that emerges when people learn with each other. Schools that treat students as passive recipients or teachers as mere implementers miss this deeper truth. Learning thrives when everyone (children, peers, parents, elders, educators) shares knowledge and insight in reciprocal exchange. When age silos dissolve, schools become ecosystems of intergenerational wisdom, curiosity, and creativity.

These ecosystems stretch beyond the walls of any single institution. Learning does not begin and end with school bells. It flows across homes, communities, workplaces, and networks, drawing strength from diversity of context. In such environments, learners practice adaptability and selfconfidence, moving easily between roles of student, mentor, and co-creator. Freed from boxes and rigid schedules, education becomes less about control and more about cultivating curiosity, resilience, and the ability to navigate complexity.

At the heart of this shift lies the fusion of agency and self-efficacy. Agency gives learners the freedom to shape their own paths. Self-efficacy gives them the belief that they can succeed. Together, they enable education to fulfill its purpose: empowering people to live with meaning, impact, and vision. Schools that prioritize both create conditions where learners are not just prepared for the future but capable of creating it.

Educators stand at the center of this transformation. They are not cogs in a machine, but creators, collaborators, and innovators. To reduce them to deliverers of outdated methods is to impoverish both learners and the future. When trusted as professionals and equipped with resources, educators become co-designers of learning environments where agency, creativity, and adaptability flourish.

If assessment remains trapped in the logic of high-stakes testing, however, none of this will be possible. Current systems reward rote memorization and anxiety while sidelining problem-solving, curiosity, and innovation. Testing culture distorts priorities, producing graduates ill-prepared for the demands of a complex world. To reimagine education, we must measure what we value (e.g., authentic growth, multi-dimensional learning, and the capacity to think critically) rather than valuing what can be most easily measured.

Technology, finally, is a mirror of these choices. Used poorly, it reproduces old practices under the illusion of modernization, wasting resources and opportunities. Used well, it expands possibilities for collaboration, creation, and deeper learning. The challenge is not the tool itself but whether we dare to transform how we learn and teach with it. The danger is in treating technology as a shortcut; the opportunity lies in developing the mindware and purposeful practices that enable it to become truly transformative.

Taken together, these commitments urge us to reimagine education as a dynamic ecosystem: intergenerational, learner-centered, educator-empowered, value-driven, and technologically purposive. Anything less leaves us trapped in the inertia of the past.

PROMPTS FOR REFLECTION

1. **Ecosystem or silo?** Identify one routine that boxes learning into rigid schedules. Redesign it to blend learning across other contexts (home, work, community, networks).

2. **Learning beyond walls**. What forms of learning in your life take place outside schools, degrees, or credentials? How do those experiences reveal the limits of institutional education?
3. **Agency + self-efficacy**. Think of a moment when you felt both free to make choices andconfident that you could succeed. What conditions made that possible, and what would it take to reproduce them at scale?
4. **Educators as innovators.** What would have to change tomorrow for educators in your context to be treated as trusted creators, not implementers? Who resists that shift, and why?
5. **The testing trap.** What is currently being measured in your school or system that actively undermines authentic learning? What would you measure instead, and how would it change behavior?
6. **Technology's mirror.** Where do you see technology being used to replicate outdated practices? How could it instead become a tool for collaboration, creation, or imagination?

Try this

Pull out a sheet of paper or use the notes pages that follow. Make a two-column list. In the first, name three things you learned in the past year that no test or metric could capture. In the second, imagine ways an institution could value those forms of learning without reducing them back into grades or scores.

Notes

Notes

Notes

INTERMEZZO
1

ACT
BUILD A POSI TIVE RE BELLION
BUILD A POSI TIVE RE BELLION
ACT
ACT
BUILD A POSI TIVE RE BELLION
ACT
BUILD A POSI TIVE RE BELLION
ACT
BUILD A POSI TIVE RE BELLION
BUILD A POSI TIVE RE BELLION
ACT

'KIDS ARE PEOPLE, TOO'
...*RIGHT*?

Some truths are so simple that we forget how demanding they are. In the context of this book, we return to one of them: *kids are people, too*. These four ordinary words are hard to oppose and yet they unsettle daily practice. Few would deny them in principle. Yet many contradict them in practice. Classrooms, playgrounds, homes, and policies often treat children as projects to be managed rather than people to be met.

Manifesto 25 states the principle without ornament. Every student is a human being with equal dignity, safety, and self-determination. Students must have real choices about their learning and their communities, bounded only by the equal rights of others. For those raised in democratic environments, this sounds obvious. For many, the discovery arrives later, and it arrives as a shock.

On August 6, 2025, a YOUDEX focus group (an Erasmus+ project aimed at promoting and exploring youth participation in democracy across Europe through digital storytelling and creative, safe digital spaces) gathered in Belgium to discuss the manifesto. The agenda listed themes and principles, but the conversation quickly turned to experience.

"It seems like common sense to me now," one participant said, "but that's not the reality. In our society, children are not treated as equals. Our opinions are ignored. Adults assume they know better." Her certainty broke when she saw corporal punishment used in front of her. "They wouldn't treat another adult like this. So why a child? It didn't make sense."

Others described smaller injuries that left longer marks. One remembered being five or six when an adult spoke to her as if she were incapable of understanding. She understood perfectly. The wound, however, came from the tone, not the words. "Even now," she said, "when I hear people talk to younger ones like that, I wonder why. They would understand if you just spoke normally." No shouting, no discipline, only dismissal. Yet the memory stayed.

Across the room the pattern repeated. Adults intended to guide experiences but ended up reducing them to small lessons. Rules meant to protect became tools of control. What appeared as order from above felt like erasure from below. The stories differed in detail and shared a common lesson: when children are not treated as people, learning shrinks to performances of obedience.

BEYOND THE STUDENT

Respect cannot stop with students. A school that claims to honor learner dignity while treating teachers as interchangeable parts hollows itself from within. One teacher from Taiwan had spent two years in a democratic school. The following year, she planned to move to a public school "to see the environment of how lonely I will be." She said it lightly, but not casually.

"If a student has different values or needs, the teacher faces obstacles,"

she explained. "You think, 'How will my colleagues see me if I give them more space?' In many schools, so much is already decided. Sometimes if you say something different, maybe the student will lose hope to create another way to go." Even in open schools, she noted, exclusion can take subtle forms. A child who struggles to communicate in expected ways may be labeled shy, lazy, or uncoöperative. "They want to join the community," she said, "but they don't have the ability or confidence yet. And there aren't enough teachers to accompany them." Her point was direct. Students cannot flourish in freedom when teachers are constrained. Teacher agency is the ground on which student agency stands.

TRUST OVER FEAR

If respect is the principle, trust is the practice. And trust does not thrive in the climate of fear that pervades so much of mainstream education. These are fear of failure, fear of disobedience, fear of anything that cannot be measured on a test.

One participant described a place that operated on a different frequency entirely: a summer camp in Belgium with only one rule: respect others and the materials. "Every week, 120 children come; different ones each time. They can do whatever they want. There's no wall, no one stopping them if they run away. But no one runs away. There's never been bullies. If you give a rule, it's like a button. People want to press it. But if you give awareness instead… they don't press it." It wasn't lawlessness. It was the kind of freedom that carries its own gravity, a shared understanding that the space exists because everyone chooses to make it work.

tion. If one falters, the rest will follow. The promise is simple. The practice is anything but. Yet in every story shared (e.g., the memory of a teacher's tone, the shock of punishment, the courage to give space, the uncelebrated success of a ruleless camp) the same truth emerges: when we act as if kids are people too, they rise to meet us as equals. And that is where the future begins.

Explore the knowledge map of the conversion.

THE LONG WORK AHEAD

Recognizing and embracing that "kids are people, too," is a long, daily discipline. It shows up in the way a teacher pauses to listen, in the trust extended to a student to make their own choice, in the willingness to change course when the current one no longer serves. It requires that we always hold open the possibility that the way we do things now is not the way we must do them tomorrow.

It is also a reminder that the culture of a school is a single ecosystem. Respect for students, respect for staff members, trust among all do not survive in isola-

12
Invisible learning is an organic process: Breathing, taking root, and becoming one's self

Most learning happens outside the frame of schooling. It appears in ordinary acts: a child testing how blocks stand, a teenager adjusting game code until it works, a retiree trading words with a neighbor to share a story. None of this requires a lesson plan. None of it needs a grade. Formal systems rarely see these moments, yet they but they form the core of how people grow. Humans learn across the whole of life, whether institutions recognize it or not.

Consider this vignette: At school, Aarya seems quiet, sometimes distracted. She struggles with spelling drills and is often told to focus harder. What her teachers do not see is what happens after school, when Aarya spends hours sketching animals from nature documentaries and inventing stories around them. She experiments with different drawing styles, researches animal habitats online, and keeps a worn notebook full of ideas for imaginary worlds. If her school logged the creative exploration she masters nightly, Aarya would already meet half the outcomes on this year's curriculum map in days.

In doing this, she develops roots of understanding (observation, narrative thinking, attention to detail, and an intuitive sense of ecosystems and relationships) nourished not by assignments, but by immersion and self-direction. This is all without a curriculum, assignments, or grades. None of it appears in her school record. But it is real learning: self-directed, deeply formative, and sustained by passion for the activity.

When a system fails to see learning beyond narrow definitions, it loses more than a data point. It loses imagination, capacity, and connection. Treating learning as something to manage rather than something to trust diminishes its power. In the rush to control growth, we strip learning of its authenticity. True education trusts learning as an organic process, emerging naturally, rooting deeply, and evolving over time, instead of forcing it into visibility.

From *Manifesto 25*:

> ***Learning happens if we attend to it or not.*** *Most learning is "invisible." It occurs outside formal instruction through informal, serendipitous experiences. It happens through curiosity, experimentation, and unplanned experiences; more like breathing than deliberate effort. Rather than forcing invisible learning into visibility, we should focus on creating environments that trust and nurture its organic flow. This means nurturing workplaces, schools, and communities that value exploration, provide opportunities to seek knowledge, and respect that not all learning needs to be measured or reported. By allowing learning to remain unseen, we preserve its authenticity and permit individuals to grow in ways that are meaningful to them. Trust, not surveillance, is the true driver of innovation and growth.*

Learning will keep happening if we allow it or not; the question is whether our systems amplify it or suffocate it.

Invisible learning refers to this continuous, often unmeasured knowledge acquisition that happens through curiosity, improvisation, and lived experience. It emerges not from formal lessons but from exploration, conversations, challenges, and moments of unexpected discovery. It is dynamic and real, even if it leaves no tidy record. Recognizing invisible learning reshapes how we understand growth: not merely as a checklist of achievements, but as a lifelong, evolving journey. As Cristóbal Cobo and I described in *Aprendizaje Invisible* (Cobo & Moravec, 2011), this phenomenon is "a continuum of learning that extends beyond formal and intentional education." It includes the unplanned discoveries made while exploring a new hobby, the critical thinking developed through informal debates with friends, and the problem-solving skills honed in daily life. Invisible learning is essential because it reflects how human beings actually live and grow: through dynamic, context-rich interactions, not isolated lessons.

Psychologist Peter Gray (2013) has shown that free play is one of the most powerful drivers of invisible learning. In unstructured, self-directed play, children practice negotiation during imaginary games, invent new rules and systems, take creative risks, resolve conflicts, and experiment with physics while building forts or obstacle courses. None of this is formally taught, however it lays the foundation for problem-solving, collaboration, creativity, and emotional resilience. Play is how young people naturally rehearse the complex skills needed for adulthood. Yet because this growth is rhizomatic, spreading beneath the surface without predictable outputs, formal systems often suppress or disregard it. By limiting free play, we are not creating more learning; we are stripping away some of the richest, most vital learning experiences people can have.

The value of invisible learning does not end in childhood. As Thomas and Brown (2011) argue, in thriving learning cultures, play, experimentation, and peer-driven exploration become primary drivers of growth—far more impactful than rigid, prescriptive instruction. Throughout life, people learn through tinkering, exploration, conversation, and spontaneous collaboration. Whether it is an amateur musician mastering new techniques through jam sessions, or a retiree learning new languages by exploring the world, learning thrives when environments support curiosity without excessive surveillance or rigid outcomes. Recognizing the role of invisible learning across all life stages challenges traditional assumptions about where learning happens, who controls it, and how it should be valued.

If we treat learning like a process to manage, we diminish it. If we treat it like breathing (vital, natural, ever-present) we begin to design schools, workplaces, and communities that allow people to grow in ways that are authentic and meaningful to them. *Trust*, not control, is the operative catalyst for innovation and growth.

When we acknowledge that the richest forms of learning often arise organically, not through force or monitoring, it becomes clear that our role is not to control learning but to create environments where it can unfold freely.

THE DANGERS OF FORCING LEARNING INTO VISIBILITY

Mainstream education relies heavily on standardized assessments, key performance indicators, and checklists to "prove" that learning or growth has occurred. As mentioned in Chapter 10, not everything that matters can be measured; and not everything that is measured matters. When curiosity is forced into outputs, when exploration is constrained into performance, and when reflection is flattened into a worksheet, something essential is lost. Learning becomes a performance, not a journey. Surveillance only stifles innovation.

This surveillance approach also erodes trust. Learners internalize that their curiosity must always be productive, that their creativity must always yield a recognizable output. In the long term, it stunts genuine innovation. People learn to perform for assessment rather than to pursue meaning, and learning shifts from being a personal journey to a series of external validations.

Knowmad Society (Moravec, 2013) warns, when education systems fail to honor informal, self-driven learning, they fail to prepare individuals for the futures they will actually inhabit, where value is increasingly created through flexibility, invention, and the ability to find meaning across contexts. In a world of rapid, unpredictable change, we cannot afford to confuse visibility with value.

Authentic growth often happens in ways we cannot see immediately: a hesitation that becomes reflection, a failed project that births a new idea, an afternoon of aimless curiosity that sparks a future calling. These moments are the heartbeat of learning.

BUILDING ENVIRONMENTS THAT EMBRACE INVISIBLE LEARNING

Learning is thus more like breathing than laborious effort. Our responsibility is not to engineer every breath, but to ensure the air is rich enough to inspire. To recognize and foster invisible learning, we must actively design environments that support its organic unfolding.

In environments that trust invisible learning:

1. Unstructured time is protected rather than rigidly filled.
2. Peer learning happens informally and is treated with respect, not suspicion.
3. Failure is seen as exploration, not a flaw or something to be punished.
4. Learners have the space to follow emerging questions without pressure for immediate, measurable outcomes.
5. Curiosity is honored on its own terms, as an end in itself.
6. Reflection takes shape through conversations, storytelling, and iterative projects, not through rigid templates.

In environments that trust invisible learning, unstructured time is protected rather than filled. Peer learning happens informally and is treated with respect, not suspicion. Failure is seen as exploration, not a flaw. Learners have the space to follow emerging questions without pressure for immediate outcomes. Curiosity is honored on its own terms. Reflection takes shape through conversations, storytelling, and iterative projects, not through rigid templates.

If we accept that much of learning is invisible, the task is not to capture or control it but to design conditions where it can thrive. Trust, not surveillance, becomes the foundation. As the OECD (2020) emphasizes, future-ready education systems must create conditions that nurture curiosity, lifelong adaptability, and informal learning opportunities across diverse contexts.

In *Aprendizaje Invisible* Cobo & Moravec (2011), we argued that learning expands when environments are rich in resources, relationships, and autonomy. People learn when they are free to ask questions, explore new tools, and connect with others across formal and informal spaces. This is less about direct instruction and more about curating ecosystems where serendipity can spark.

Practically, this means:

- **In schools**, redesigning spaces to encourage unstructured time: maker spaces, flexible commons, outdoor classrooms, and studio environments where learners can follow questions wherever they lead. It means valuing inquiry over compliance, dialogue over recitation, and portfolios of personal work over standardized tests.

- **In workplaces**, encouraging experimentation, allowing for "intelligent failure" without punishment, and creating informal spaces (e.g., lounges, workshops, and virtual forums) where knowledge can circulate organically across roles and disciplines.
- **In communities**, designing civic spaces that invite people of different ages and backgrounds to collaborate, share, and experiment. Public libraries, hackerspaces, and urban gardens are natural laboratories of invisible learning, where discovery happens without a syllabus. UNESCO (2021) similarly calls for a new social contract for education, one that moves beyond schools as isolated spaces and recognizes learning as a lifelong, interconnected, and community-driven process.

Building for invisible learning means shifting the role of the educator, manager, or leader from controller to cultivator. It requires believing that people, when trusted, will grow. Not always predictably. Not always immediately. But authentically, and in ways that ultimately nourish more resilient, inventive, and fulfilled individuals.

Learning was never meant to occur in cages. It breathes in conversations, roots itself in moments of curiosity, and grows through the soil and varied landscape of lived experience. When we stop chasing old ideas and start cultivating possibility, learning returns to what it has always been: an act of becoming. The task ahead is to create places rich enough, wild enough, and human enough for it to breathe.

13
We cannot manage knowledge

Education often mistakes *knowledge* for *information*, reducing learning to the storage and recall of facts. Students are tested on their ability to recall information, not on their depth of understanding. However, memorization is not the same as knowledge. Learning is a process of transformation, not just accumulation. To make sense of the world, students must move beyond collecting data and information to constructing knowledge. True innovation happens only when they take what they know and use it to create new meaning and value. Understanding these distinctions reveals a core flaw in education. Schools excel at managing information, but they cannot manage knowledge without reducing it back into information.

From *Manifesto 25*:

> ***Knowledge is constructed from meaning, not management.*** *When we talk about knowledge and innovation, we frequently commingle or confuse the concepts with data and information instead. Too often, we fool ourselves into thinking that we give learners "knowledge" when we are just testing them for the rote recall of information. To be clear:* **Data** *are bits and pieces here and there, from which we combine into* **information**. **Knowledge** *is about taking information and creating meaning at a personal level. We* **innovate** *when we take action with what we know to create new value. Understanding this difference exposes one of the greatest problems facing school management and teaching: While we are good at managing information, we simply cannot manage the knowledge in students' heads without degrading it back to information.*

Breaking this down further:

- **Data** consists of raw facts, numbers, and details that, on their own, lack meaning. A student can see historical dates, scientific measurements, or mathematical figures, but without context, these pieces remain disconnected. Schools often bombard students with data, assuming exposure alone leads to understanding. But data is only a starting point. Without a framework for interpretation, it is just noise. Memorizing statistics about climate change does not mean grasping its causes or consequences.

- **Information** is created when data is structured and organized. It provides context and patterns, helping learners connect facts. A timeline of historical events or a graph showing temperature trends turns scattered data into something understandable. Schools operate mostly at this level, delivering structured content through textbooks, lectures, and assessments. But information remains static until it is personally engaged with. Understanding does not come from receiving information but from actively working with it: questioning, applying, and reshaping information to make sense.

- **Knowledge** emerges when individuals internalize information and attach meaning to it. Unlike data or information, it cannot be passively received; it must be actively constructed. A student may memorize the formula for acceleration, but until they apply it to solve a real-world problem, they have not gained knowledge. The same applies to history, literature, and every other subject. Facts alone do not create understanding. Knowledge requires engagement, personal interpretation, and the ability to apply ideas in different contexts. This is where education often fails. Schools can manage information by delivering lessons and grading tests, but they cannot control how or whether students turn information into knowledge.

- **Innovation** emerges when knowledge is applied to generate new ideas, solve problems, and create value. It is the application of understanding in new ways. It cannot be standardized, scripted, or mass-produced. Innovation is unpredictable, emerging from curiosity, experimentation, and synthesis. A student who deeply understands a concept is not limited to repeating it. They can adapt it, question it, and use it to drive new discoveries. Schools often claim to promote innovation, but rigid structures that prioritize compliance and repetition over creativity stifle this potential. Real innovation requires an environment where learners are free to explore, take risks, and push beyond existing knowledge.

Schools organize and deliver information efficiently, yet they cannot control how students internalize it. Knowledge is personal and develops through experience, reflection, and engagement. When education tries to standardize knowledge, it strips away meaning and reduces learning to the recall of information. Tests can measure what students remember, but they cannot capture how well they understand, apply, or create new ideas.

The more schools attempt to fit knowledge into predefined structures, the more they turn it into information that can be categorized, tested, and managed. Standardized assessments prioritize memorization and compliance over curiosity, creativity, and critical thinking. They measure institutional efficiency, not genuine understanding (Shepard, 2000; Koretz, 2017).

THIS IS FOR THE BENEFIT OF THE SCHOOL, BUT SAYS NOTHING OF WHAT STUDENTS ACTUALLY KNOW.

TOWARDS KNOWLEDGE CREATION:
A PROCESS-ORIENTED APPROACH

To foster knowledge creation and innovation, schools must rethink how learning happens. Instead of treating students as passive recipients of content, education should encourage exploration, problem-solving, and interdisciplinary thinking. This requires shifting from rigid instruction to dynamic learning environments where students actively construct meaning.

Schools should prioritize inquiry-based learning that values questions as much as answers. When students solve real problems instead of memorizing facts, they engage with knowledge in a more meaningful way (Hmelo-Silver, 2004). Open-ended exploration, discussion, and learning through mistakes help them refine their understanding rather than absorb fixed conclusions.

Assessment should move beyond standardized testing to focus on how students apply their knowledge. Project-based evaluations, portfolios, and presentations allow students to use information in novel ways and demonstrate deeper understanding (Schute & Becker, 2010). As noted in chapter 10, learning is not about accumulating facts but about making connections and generating ideas.

Collaboration should take precedence over competition. Knowledge grows through dialogue, iteration, and the exchange of perspectives. Schools should encourage collaborative learning environments where students challenge ideas, refine their thinking, and develop solutions together. Cross-disciplinary projects, peer feedback, and partnerships with universities and industry expand learning beyond rote absorption into active knowledge creation.

Education is a process, not a product. A *product* is designed for consistency, quality control, and uniformity in its final form. It follows a blueprint with predefined specifications, ensuring that each iteration closely resembles the last. But learning does not work this way. Knowledge cannot be mass-produced, and understanding cannot be standardized without stripping away its depth and significance. Every learner engages with information in a unique way, bringing their own experiences, interpretations, and questions to the process. When education is treated as a fixed product, students are expected to arrive at the same conclusions in the same way, leaving little room for creativity, discovery, or independent thought.

A *process*, by contrast, embraces unpredictability and transformation. It values exploration, allowing for outcomes that cannot always be anticipated or measured. Authentic learning does not follow a linear path from instruction to mastery. It is shaped by experimentation, curiosity, and the connections students make along the way. This openness to the unknown is what allows for the emergence of new knowledge and innovation. If education is to move beyond rote instruction, it must cultivate environments where students are not just consumers of information but active participants in meaning-making. When learning is seen as a dynamic and evolving process, students are free to engage with ideas in ways that lead to breakthroughs, new perspectives, and creative solutions that no curriculum could have predicted.

Knowledge-building is a process that is attended to, not managed. Innovation thrives when students have the freedom to pursue their interests and explore ideas without rigid constraints. Allowing them to design their own projects, conduct self-directed research, and integrate multiple disciplines into their learning helps them develop knowledge instead of merely receiving information.

Achieving this profound transformation from information management to knowledge creation hinges on deliberate changes to educational infrastructure. This includes investing in teacher professional development that prioritizes facilitation, mentorship, and the design of inquiry-based experiences, rather than content mastery. It also requires the adoption of flexible curriculum frameworks and assessment models that encourage exploration and application over rote memorization, supported by administrative policies that empower innovation at every level.

Shifting from information management to knowledge creation requires a fundamental change in education. Schools must prioritize thinking over testing, inquiry over instruction, and creativity over compliance. They must redefine success, not by how much a student can recall, but by what they can do with what they know. Educators should foster environments where knowledge can grow, not control it. Only then can schools move beyond managing information and fulfill the true purpose of learning: creating knowledge and driving innovation.

14

Toward creative futures, beyond standardization

Standardization prioritizes predictability over possibility, compliance over creativity, and repetition over risk-taking. When education reduces students to manufactured products, it ignores their unique potential to seek out their own passions and solve problems creatively. Rigid curricula measure success through narrow tests and predetermined outcomes, suffocating curiosity and limiting students' abilities to navigate complexities of the real world.

The world no longer rewards uniformity. Critical thinking and creativity are crucial. Machines can handle routine work. Education should not produce routine sameness. It should cultivate possibility. Learning organizations must replace conformity with flexibility and design environments that invite exploration, experimentation, and original thinking. Creativity and innovation emerge when learners have permission to follow their interests, collaborate across boundaries, and engage with problems that matter (Brynjolfsson & McAffee, 2014).

From *Manifesto 25*:

> ***Standardization kills creativity and innovation.*** *One-size-fits-all education turns learners into uniform outputs, measuring success through narrow assessments. By fragmenting knowledge into isolated subjects, it overlooks the complexity of real-world challenges and curbs experimentation and bold thinking. To foster genuine innovation, we must abandon rigid uniformity and adopt adaptive, learner-centered approaches that emphasize open-ended inquiry and interdisciplinary*

collaboration. Only when students can explore their interests, exchange diverse perspectives, and engage in authentic problem-solving does true creativity flourish.

THE HIDDEN COSTS OF STANDARDIZED EDUCATION

Standardization disproportionately impacts students from marginalized or underrepresented groups by enforcing narrow definitions of success. Students whose experiences, cultural perspectives, or ways of thinking differ from standardized norms are often disadvantaged, their creative abilities undervalued or overlooked entirely. Such educational inequities reinforce broader social inequalities by limiting who is recognized as successful (Darling-Hammond, 2010). An equitable education system must ensure diverse forms of creativity and innovation are encouraged and valued, affirming the strengths of all learners rather than rewarding conformity.

By the time something becomes standardized, it typically reflects outdated concepts or priorities disconnected from contemporary needs. Standardized curricula rarely keep pace with rapid technological, social, and economic changes, leaving students ill-prepared for the dynamic demands of the modern world. This misalignment reinforces learning approaches based on conformity rather than creativity, leading to outdated educational outcomes.

Rigid curricula and standardized tests reward uniformity rather than originality. Pressure to meet standardized benchmarks discourages risk-taking and penalizes experimentation (both critical to meaningful learning and innovation). Consequently, schools produce learners skilled in following directions yet challenged by ambiguity, complexity, and novel situations.

The cost of conformity in education is high. When learning institutions prioritize uniformity, they inadvertently discourage intellectual curiosity and experimentation. Students conditioned for conformity become hesitant to question established ideas, fearful of straying from the correct answers outlined by standardized curricula. Over time, this discourages creativity, limits innovation, and narrows the range of ideas learners feel comfortable expressing.

The outcome is a generation of students who can reproduce knowledge but struggle to originate it, precisely when society demands innovators capable of responding to evolving global challenges (Zhao, 2012; Sawyer, 2012).

Furthermore, conformity-driven education exacerbates existing inequities. Students whose cultural backgrounds, interests, or learning styles differ from standardized expectations often face disadvantages, feeling marginalized when their strengths remain unrecognized or devalued. This undermines equity by rewarding sameness rather than celebrating diverse talents and approaches to learning. Reducing conformity in education is therefore critical to ensuring fairness and supporting every learner's unique contributions.

CULTIVATING CREATIVITY: PILLARS OF AN ADAPTIVE LEARNING SYSTEM

Real-world problems rarely fit neatly into traditional academic categories. Yet schools often compartmentalize knowledge into isolated disciplines, separating science from art, mathematics from humanities, and theory from practice. This fragmentation prevents students from appreciating the interconnected nature of real-life challenges, hindering their ability to develop comprehensive and innovative solutions (Klein, 2015).

A learner-centered approach replaces rigid standards with personalized learning paths. Students explore their interests through inquiry driven by curiosity and authentic questions. Educators facilitate interdisciplinary projects enabling students to integrate knowledge, collaborate with peers, and develop solutions to meaningful issues. Such an environment encourages experimentation, critical thinking, and creative risk-taking, fostering innovation rather than replication of established knowledge. This approach also advances equity by recognizing diverse ways of learning and providing all students, especially marginalized learners, equal opportunities to engage and succeed.

A learner-centered education moves beyond predetermined outcomes, allowing students to engage deeply with questions and problems meaningful to them. Students become active participants in defining their educational journeys, guided by their curiosity rather than standardized benchmarks.

In practice, this approach involves flexible curricula that adapt to students' evolving interests and real-world concerns. Learners engage in inquiry-driven projects and research, supported by educators who act as facilitators rather than mere dispensers of content. Such environments nurture students' intrinsic motivation, creative capacities, and self-direction—skills vital for adapting to future challenges.

Interdisciplinary collaboration significantly enhances creativity and innovation. When students work across disciplinary boundaries, they learn to view problems from multiple perspectives, uncovering connections and solutions a single subject lens might miss. Integrating disciplines like art with engineering or literature with technology helps students develop original and effective approaches to complex tasks, reflecting the collaborative nature of contemporary innovation.

Interdisciplinary education enriches students' intellectual experiences and prepares them to address the increasingly complex, multifaceted problems of today. Challenges such as climate change, public health crises, and social inequalities require integrated approaches combining science, technology, humanities, and arts. Traditional education, organized by isolated subjects, struggles to provide students with these skills. Embracing interdisciplinary learning means providing structured opportunities (e.g., collaborative problem-solving, community projects, or design-based challenges) to encourage students to think across boundaries and develop holistic solutions. Such collaboration fosters innovative thinking by encouraging students to combine diverse perspectives and methods.

Assessment methods should align directly with the skills and qualities education aims to develop. Authentic assessments (e.g., portfolios, project presentations, or real-world problem-solving activities) better capture students' capacities for innovation, critical thinking, and application of knowledge in diverse contexts. These assessments encourage iterative learning and improvement, emphasizing growth rather than fearing mistakes. Measuring what truly matters ensures that creativity and meaningful innovation are recognized and valued (Shute & Becker, 2010).

Traditional standardized assessments emphasize memorization, speed, and compliance, sidelining deeper, more meaningful forms of learning. They measure narrow academic skills, neglecting essential capabilities like creativity, collaboration, critical thinking, and resilience. These are things that are already being replaced by AI in the workplace and society. Such limited assessments create incentives for teachers and students to focus on test preparation at the expense of genuine exploration and understanding. The consequence is a system that values surface-level recall over authentic skill development and innovation, contrary to what students genuinely need for long-term success.

IF WE MUST STICK TO A STANDARDIZED SYSTEM, LET'S GET PRACTICAL …

In most industrialized regimes, standardization is unavoidable. In such cases, policymakers should consider flexible approaches similar to Minnesota's Profile of Learning from the late 1990s (see DeLapp, 2008). Unlike traditional rigid standards, this approach emphasized practical skills, critical thinking, and interdisciplinary, project-based learning. Students were evaluated through authentic assessments such as portfolios and performance tasks that demonstrated real-world application of knowledge. Policymakers and educators should adopt similar flexible standards today, ensuring consistency without sacrificing creativity or innovation. Recommended policies include integrating project-based assessments, encouraging interdisciplinary curricula, and maintaining sufficient flexibility to allow students and teachers to pursue individual interests and address contemporary societal challenges. Specifically, policymakers should adopt frameworks prioritizing authentic assessment methods, project-based curricula, and student-led inquiry, providing practical models for equitable education reform. Adopting this policy approach can balance accountability with meaningful, student-centered learning experiences.

Several current education systems illustrate how flexible standardization can successfully balance accountability with creativity and innovation:

Finland's national curriculum framework

Finland's education system uses flexible national standards focusing on interdisciplinary learning, critical thinking, and real-world problem-solving. Students regularly collaborate on projects across subject areas, assessed through authentic tasks rather than standardized exams.

Expeditionary Learning (USA)

EL Education schools use performance-based assessments and portfolios instead of standardized tests. Students engage in community-based, interdisciplinary projects with an emphasis on problem-solving, collaboration, and presentation skills, reflecting a balanced approach to standards.

British Columbia's redesigned curriculum (Canada)

British Columbia's curriculum emphasizes personalized learning and competency-based assessments, promoting deeper thinking and innovation. Assessments prioritize student portfolios, self-assessments, and demonstrations of applied skills and knowledge.

Educational leaders must advocate for curricula flexibility, interdisciplinary learning opportunities, and assessments that recognize diverse achievements. Moving away from uniformity allows schools to unlock students' creative potential, enabling them to adapt, innovate, and thrive amid uncertainty. Shifting from standardization towards adaptive learning approaches aligns closely with *Manifesto 25*'s call for commiting to equity, creativity, and preparing students effectively for future challenges.

In embracing creativity over rigid standards, education transforms from transactional to transformative. Learners gain freedom to explore interests, collaborate across disciplines, and engage meaningfully with complex problems. This approach supports equitable learning opportunities, preparing all students to positively shape (and lead) their futures.

15

Learning at the edge of networks

In early 2020, as COVID-19 spread across the globe, the limits of isolated expertise became clear. No single discipline, institution, or government could respond alone. Progress depended on convergence. Diverse perspectives, rapid experimentation, and global collaboration combined to generate new knowledge at speed. Much of the most consequential learning happened between institutions, not within them, as ideas moved quickly across boundaries and adapted to local needs.

Open networks and platforms became connective tissue. On GitHub, developers collaborated on pandemic models and tracing apps. Makerspaces 3D-printed personal protective equipment (PPE) and shared files freely. Wikipedia editors updated thousands of entries in dozens of languages. Teachers traded lesson plans across social media and adapted them for their communities.

What made this response so powerful was the way networks allowed people to bring their knowledge, constructed from personal and institutional meanings derived from data and information, into conversation with others. A mechanical engineer in Nairobi, a biology teacher in São Paulo, and a community health organizer in New Delhi could all engage meaningfully in shared learning experiences, each contributing and adapting ideas to fit their own contexts. Together, they generated knowledge that was richer than the sum of its parts.

The COVID-19 response reminded us knowledge is not static, nor does it live solely in experts or textbooks. It grows where boundaries are crossed between disciplines, cultures, and lived experiences. This type of learning thrives at the edges of systems, where insights collide and new meanings emerge. In an interconnected world, the agency and developed self-efficacy to navigate these intersections is crucial.

INTERSECTING NETWORKS MAKE KNOWLEDGE VISIBLE

When we say knowledge grows at the boundaries of networks, we mean more than information exchange. We mean *transformative new knowledge production*: where something new and valuable emerges through the encounter between perspectives. Knowledge becomes visible when perspectives collide and produce value that did not exist before. It moves across people, places, and ideas, gathering strength as it goes.

From *Manifesto 25*:

> ***Knowledge grows where the boundaries of networks intersect.*** *The emerging pedagogy of this century isn't carefully planned—it evolves fluidly. Learning unfolds as we traverse and expand networks, connecting individual knowledge to create new understandings. By sharing experiences, we generate social knowledge that enriches collective insight. Education must prioritize equipping individuals with the tools, competencies, and literacies (such as digital fluency, cultural awareness, and network navigation) needed to thrive in these interconnected systems. Through this process, learners contextualize their unique talents and knowledge, empowering them to tackle new challenges with creativity and confidence.*

This view aligns with earlier discussions of invisible learning, where growth often unfolds without formal scripts or recognition. Self-directed work becomes powerful when it intersects with shared spaces and tools. Learning also gains strength when education moves beyond rigid containers and reflects the fluidity of life outside classrooms. It does not begin or end on schedule. It deepens where communities and experiences overlap.

The fusion of agency and self-efficacy further expands this view. When people are trusted to navigate their own networks (i.e., to make choices, experiment, and persist) they transcend learning to become contributors. Agency enables exploration, and self-efficacy fuels the belief that one's contributions matter. Together, these forces position learners as nodes in living networks, not as passive consumers of information.

This has profound implications. In a world shaped by overlapping crises and complex challenges, knowledge confined to silos is insufficient. We need people who can translate insights between domains, bridge unfamiliar contexts, and ask better questions. Whether we are talking about climate adaptation, digital governance, or community resilience, it is at these points of intersection (across disciplines, generations, and geographies) that real learning accelerates and new knowledge is born.

FRAMEWORKS FOR LEARNING AT THE EDGE OF NETWORKS

To design education for a networked world, we need frameworks that reflect how knowledge forms, not as static content to be consumed, but as a phenomena that is dynamic, relational, and constructed from co-created meaning. This requires us to rethink not only pedagogical methods, but the very architecture of learning systems.

One useful model is the connectivist framework proposed by George Siemens (2007b) and Stephen Downes (2022). Connectivism suggests that learning in the digital age is no longer about what we know individually, but about how we connect to knowledge distributed across networks, both human and technological. The ability to recognize patterns, locate expertise, and build knowledge socially becomes more important than memorizing facts. In this model, educators act less as content experts and more as network facilitators: helping learners identify, join, and contribute to communities of practice.

The rhizomatic learning model, inspired by Deleuze and Guattari (1987), offers another lens. It sees learning as an unpredictable, self-propagating process that grows like a rhizome, nonlinear, with multiple entry and exit points. In this model, the role of curriculum is not to prescribe paths, but to invite exploration, improvisation, and co-construction. Knowledge emerges not from authority, but from participation.

We can also draw from knowledge building theory (Scardamalia & Bereiter, 2010), which positions learning communities as agents of collective cognitive advancement. Learners are expected to not only absorb ideas, but to advance them. The goal is not just understanding existing knowledge, but improving it. Central to this is the principle of epistemic agency: learners take responsibility for identifying problems, generating ideas, and refining them through dialogue and feedback.

Table 1. Overview of network learning frameworks.

FRAMEWORK	CORE IDEA	ROLE OF LEARNER	ROLE OF EDUCATOR	IMPACT
Connectivism	Learning happens through connections across people and digital systems	Navigates, synthesizes, participates in communities	Facilitates connections, curates resources	Prioritizes digital fluency and knowledge navigation
Rhizomatic learning	Knowledge grows unpredictably through exploration	Co-constructs meaning through open inquiry	Creates conditions for improvisation	Encourages adaptive, nonlinear learning paths
Knowledge building	Learning communities improve collective understanding	Advances ideas collaboratively, takes epistemic agency	Guides inquiry, supports knowledge refinement	Builds capacity for sustained innovation and social learning

These frameworks are united by a core tenent that knowledge thrives at the edges when people, contexts, and experiences collide and collaborate. In practice, this means designing learning experiences that:

1. Encourage boundary-crossing: working across disciplines, age groups, cultures, and roles.
2. Center inquiry: framing learning around meaningful, complex questions rather than fixed content.
3. Promote network literacy: helping learners navigate digital spaces, identify trustworthy sources, and build collaborative knowledge online.
4. Invite participation: ensuring learners have voice, choice, and responsibility in shaping their learning environments.

5. Value iteration: understanding knowledge as always evolving, provisional, and in need of refinement through dialogue and action.

As we design systems to support this kind of learning, we must move away from rigid hierarchies and toward structures that are open, relational, and adaptable. The aim is not to master a body of knowledge, but to become fluent in the movement of knowledge itself.

LEARNING AT THE INTERSECTIONS

In a world defined by flux, complexity, and deep interdependence, knowledge moves across networks, communities, and platforms: growing, mutating, and adapting through every new connection each of us make. To educate for such a world, we must stop treating learning as a transfer of static content and start embracing it as a generative, social, and networked practice. When education helps learners find the edges of their knowledge and connect with others across disciplines, backgrounds, and lived experience, something transformative happens. Individual insight becomes collective intelligence. Personal growth contributes to shared capacity. The purpose of learning shifts from preparing people to fit into predefined roles toward preparing them to help shape what comes next.

This is at the heart of the message of *Manifesto 25*: learning does not evolve through coercion and control, but through authentic contact. Through relationships. Through friction, divergence, and shared creation. And that knowledge, at its most beneficial, is something that emerges from our shared experiences. Designing for this kind of learning doesn't mean discarding structure, but building systems that are flexible enough to adapt, open enough to connect, and brave enough to trust in emergence. In these systems, learners extend what they know, remix what is known by others, and share new knowledge and innovative outputs to bring change into the world.

Education thus becomes an act of weaving: drawing together people, ideas, and tools across space and time. At every intersection, new possibilities emerge for creativity, for understanding, and for transformative action.

16

Degrees are obsolete by design...
when knowledge has the shelf life of a banana

Rapid advances in science, technology, and the organization of work have shortened the lifespan of knowledge. A university degree can lose relevance faster than a banana browns on a kitchen counter. The familiar script of earn a diploma, secure a career, follow a stable path no longer fits present conditions. This shift marks a clear break from prior expectations about stability in knowledge and work in an *Age of Disruption*. Knowledge that once remained stable long enough to anchor four-year programs now changes within a single cohort. Students often find that what they learned in their first year needs revision before the second year begins (Reich, 2020).

This pattern is widely recognized by educators, innovators, and futurists who see the speed of change reshaping how learning works (see esp. World Economic Forum, 2025). The question is no longer whether disciplines such as science, technology, engineering, or the humanities are transforming, but how quickly and how deeply. Static curricula struggle to keep pace. In response, forward-looking voices argue for learning experiences that remain fluid and adaptive, aligned with emerging technologies and shifting social needs. Their conclusion is blunt. The diploma, as we know it, is overdue for retirement.

As we wrote in *Manifesto 25*:

> ***Degrees are obsolete by design.*** *Many static degree programs, designed for fixed fields with clear endpoints, are outdated or obsolete before students even finish their first year. Traditional diplomas fail to keep up with accelerating change and often do not capture the depth of real-world skills and achievements. A concerted shift toward a new, decentralized system is needed that values creativity, problem-solving, and real impact over time spent in a classroom. Learners need dynamic recognition systems that adapt with them, rewarding growth and contributions that reflect the ever-changing demands of the world.*

A degree in chemical engineering or marketing presumed a stable body of knowledge and practice. But as we race forward, these fields can morph into something unrecognizable within a few short years. Traditional diplomas cannot keep up; they are an artifact of a slower age, more adept at signaling seat time than demonstrating genuine, future-ready skills.

In the Age of Disruption, adaptability and imagination matter more than static credentials. We may be approaching what has been called a *technological singularity* (Vinge, 1992), but the more immediate limit may be human imagination itself. Can we anticipate the possibilities that lie beyond our current capacity to predict? As machines learn, industries reorganize, and new challenges surface, the most reliable asset is not a fixed credential, but a learning mindset that keeps pace with change or even moves ahead of it (Dweck, 2006).

Yet this is not a doomsday scenario. It is an impulse to rethink what "qualification" means. We need new approaches, interacting within a decentralized system that places creativity, problem-solving, and tangible impact above classroom hours. Instead of pointing to a diploma as proof of mastery, learners should be able to showcase evolving portfolios of projects, innovations, and collaborations that demonstrate they can thrive under uncertainty. Failing, pivoting, and experimenting become necessary rites of passage, not black marks.

In such systems, educators shift roles. They become curators and facilitators who guide learners through personalized pathways rather than enforce standardized sequences. Formal credentials may still matter, but they must remain dynamic. Learners should be able to advance in real time, based on demonstrated capability, rather than wait for a single ceremony or diploma that declares learning complete. No one ever finishes learning.

So, what do we do when a university degree has the shelf life of a banana? We embrace radical reinvention. We stop treating education as a box to check and start seeing it as a continuous, creative process that extends beyond campus walls and transcends narrow disciplinary boundaries. We expand our definition of intelligence to include emotional resilience, ethical reasoning, and collaborative capacity. We harness the human ability to reinvent ourselves; and in doing so, we find new possibilities even as the horizon keeps shifting.

FIVE PATHWAYS BEYOND DIPLOMAS FOLLOW THIS SHIFT:

1. Rethinking credentialing through dynamic portfolios.

One way to move beyond static degrees is to adopt continuous, real-time assessment models that grow with learners. Instead of earning a diploma at the end of a fixed program, individuals build dynamic portfolios that showcase their evolving capabilities. As they complete projects, collaborate on teams, or develop new solutions, these achievements are added to a living profile accessible to employers, peers, and educational institutions. This approach values a learner's ongoing growth rather than confining their accomplishments to a single piece of paper, and it offers transparent evidence of what they can contribute in a rapidly changing environment. Portfolios carry one's work beyond graduation.

2. Embracing micro-credentials and open badges.

In a decentralized learning ecosystem, formal credentials can still serve a purpose, if they are flexible enough to adapt. Micro-credentials or digital badges awarded for specific skills, accomplishments, and contributions provide a more granular view of a learner's journey. A software developer might accumulate badges for expertise in emerging coding frameworks, while a social worker might earn credentials in specialized counseling methods. These smaller, targeted recognitions reflect genuine progress and demonstrate readiness for real-world challenges, whether they occur within or outside traditional institutions.

3. Peer review and collaborative validation.

Learners often rely on instructors or administrators to validate their progress, but a strong alternative is to adopt collaborative models of feedback and assessment. In a "flat" educational structure, feedback flows freely among peers, mentors, and community members who have direct insight into a learner's contributions. This approach mimics real-world teamwork, where successful outcomes depend on collective input. Platforms that facilitate peer review and group reflection can create a culture of continuous improvement, reducing reliance on top-down authority while empowering learners to refine their skills in immediate, meaningful ways.

4. Integrating human-centered technology.

Technology can streamline these innovations and make them scalable. Decentralized, blockchain-based networks, for example, offer a secure way to track achievements without a central gatekeeper. Learners can store their credentials in a personal digital wallet, which remains valid across different institutions and industries. Meanwhile, AI-driven recommendation systems can help learners identify areas for growth, serving as personalized "learning navigators." These technologies don't replace human guidance but enhance it, freeing educators to focus on personalized mentorship, well-being, and complex problem-solving rather than administrative tasks.

5. Moving from "one and done" to lifelong learning.

Perhaps the most significant shift is recognizing that nobody ever truly finishes learning. Degrees traditionally imply an endpoint, but in a world where technology and social realities are perpetually in flux, education must remain fluid and continuous. Institutions can become hubs for life-long learning, offering frequent "level-ups" that reflect new competencies earned through work, service, or independent research. The real question is not whether a person has a diploma, but how they continue to develop their capabilities and how their growth is recognized and shared.

The assumption that an intensive burst of study early in life is enough to equip us for decades of work no longer holds. Our world evolves too quickly, and the pace of innovation demands continuous skill-building and re-skilling well beyond a two- or four-year program. Education must expand its scope to become a lifelong process rather than a single "one and done" credential. This requires a fundamental shift in both structure and purpose: rather than institutions that primarily serve eighteen-year-olds on a campus, we need fluid networks that support learners of all ages, with flexible entry points, schedules, and curricula that adapt to changing industry and societal needs. Such a model breaks away from the notion of finishing your education by a certain age and encourages people to view learning as an ongoing, iterative journey.

When education is dispersed throughout life, it challenges the term "higher education" as we know it. If universities become hubs for ongoing growth rather than a single phase, we may need to find new language that goes beyond "continuing education," "distributed education," or even "learning ecosystems." The implications are significant. Funding models, accreditation processes, and campus infrastructure would all need a complete overhaul. The student-faculty relationship might become more fluid, with learners entering and leaving structured programs repeatedly over the course of their careers. Faculty themselves may take on more roles as coaches, project collaborators, co-learners and community organizers, rather than traditional lecturers. This transformation would also demand technological tools that seamlessly integrate lived experience, work outcomes, and project-based achievements into ongoing assessments of skill and knowledge. The result would be a fundamentally different conception of education: one that stays relevant no matter where you are in life, or how quickly the world changes around you.

This moment calls for imagination unbound by old norms. *Manifesto 25* frames this not as rejection for its own sake, but as an affirmation of possibility. When education values growth over stasis, impact over seat time, and creative courage over predictability, it becomes capable of meeting a future that refuses to stand still.

CAHIER THREE

Learning as human and relational

FRAMING

Learning unfolds whether we notice it or not. Much of it is invisible, woven into daily experience through curiosity, experimentation, and encounters beyond the classroom. Attempts to force this kind of learning into visibility strip it of its vitality. The core task is to create spaces of trust—schools, workplaces, and communities that value exploration, support growth, and do not confuse measurement with meaning.

At the same time, education often mistakes information for knowledge. Data and facts can be gathered, stored, and tested, but they become knowledge only when individuals create meaning and use it to act in the world. Efforts to "manage" knowledge reduce it back into fragments, undermining the possibility of innovation.

Standardization deepens this problem. One-size-fits-all schooling flattens diversity, fragments understanding into isolated subjects, and rewards uniform outputs over imagination. Genuine creativity depends on open inquiry, the freedom to cross boundaries, and opportunities to connect ideas in unexpected ways.

The future of learning lies in networks. As individuals share what they know, intersections generate new insights and collective growth. Navigating these networks requires literacies such as digital fluency, cultural awareness, and the ability to collaborate across contexts. Education must prepare learners to thrive in these interconnected spaces, not in static silos.

Traditional degrees, designed for stable fields and fixed outcomes, no longer match the pace of change. Many lose relevance before students even graduate, failing to capture real skills and contributions. What is needed is a new system of recognition that evolves with learners, values creativity and problem-solving, and reflects impact in the real world rather than time spent in a classroom.

This third cahier is an invitation to reimagine education beyond its current frame: to respect the invisible, treat knowledge as meaning, reject uniformity, embrace networks, and design recognition systems that move with us.

PROMPTS FOR REFLECTION

1. **Invisible learning.** Recall a moment when you learned something vital outside school or work structures. How did it change you? Why would traditional education struggle to recognize it?
2. **Information vs. knowledge.** Where in your learning are you rewarded for recalling fragments instead of creating meaning? What is lost when education treats information as an endpoint?
3. **Uniformity vs. creativity.** How has standardization flattened your own learning or that of people around you? What could replace one-size-fits-all schooling with approaches that honor difference and imagination?
4. **Networks as classrooms.** Which networks (digital, cultural, professional, social) have most expanded your horizons? How might schools and institutions embrace those intersections instead of pretending they do not exist?
5. **Degrees by design.** If diplomas are already obsolete by the time they are granted, what forms of recognition could capture the real skills, creativity, and impact of learners today?
6. **Trust as infrastructure.** What would it take for your school, workplace, or community to create environments of deep trust where invisible learning can thrive without being forced into metrics?

Try this

Pull out a sheet of paper or use the notes pages that follow. Sketch a recognition system that would credit what you actually create, share, or contribute in networks of learning. Show how it values growth without collapsing it back into grades or credentials.

Notes

Notes

Notes

17

Genuine equity demands creative schools

Education systems that define success through conformity and compliance perpetuate inequity by design. This narrow framing sidelines learners whose strengths lie in originality, invention, or unconventional thinking. Students who solve problems differently or express ideas in nontraditional ways are overlooked or mislabeled. Equity cannot exist in systems that reward sameness. True equity requires recognizing and valuing a wide range of talents, perspectives, and lived experiences, and dismantling the structures that suppress creative expression and innovative thought.

From *Manifesto 25*:

> *Any education system that tolerates inequities is complicit in injustice. Systems designed to perpetuate inequality fail everyone. Schools must move beyond token acknowledgments of diversity to dismantle systemic barriers. Curricula should amplify marginalized voices and ensure that every learner is genuinely seen, heard, and valued. Equity and inclusion are not optional add-ons—they are the foundation of a fair and sustainable education system.*

Genuine equity takes shape in learning environments where students are trusted to explore and express creativity without fear. This matters most for learners who have been discouraged or excluded because of race, gender, socioeconomic status, disability, or intersecting identities. Inclusive schools understand creativity as central to learning, not a distraction from it. They create conditions where students feel safe experimenting, asking unfamiliar questions, and developing perspectives that challenge convention. In these environments, learners are empowered to shape futures that reflect who they are (Gay, 2018).

An equitable school culture invites experimentation and intellectual risk. Teachers model curiosity, welcome divergence, and actively seek out perspectives that are often ignored. This approach is especially powerful for students of color, students from lower-income backgrounds, students with disabilities, and others marginalized by rigid educational norms. When creativity is treated as a core value, schools acknowledge that talent is distributed widely, even when opportunity is not (see esp. Robinson, 2011).

Curricula that prioritize creativity elevate marginalized voices by design. When students are encouraged to generate original work, their identities, cultures, and experiences become part of the curriculum itself. Creative learning moves beyond surface-level diversity and integrates lived experience into daily practice. Inclusion means creating spaces where students can speak from who they are, even when their perspectives unsettle established assumptions.

Equity ultimately requires moving away from rigid standards toward flexible, personalized learning pathways that align with each learner's strengths, interests, and context. Personalized approaches benefit students from marginalized communities by expanding what success looks like. Achievement can emerge through art, science, entrepreneurship, civic action, or social innovation. When education recognizes multiple pathways, it honors intersectional identities and fosters belonging, engagement, and purpose (Zhao, 2012).

School leaders and policymakers can take concrete steps to advance equity through creativity and innovation.

1. Redesign curricula for interdisciplinary creativity and inclusion.

Curricula should prioritize interdisciplinary exploration, project-based learning, and real-world problem-solving. Students might tackle sustainability by using digital tools and data analytics to propose innovative solutions for their communities. Lessons should leverage diverse cultural experiences, inviting students to express ideas through digital media, coding, and storytelling platforms. For example, students might use digital storytelling platforms and data analytics to document and analyze local community histories, allowing them to amplify traditionally marginalized voices, experiences, and perspectives while developing digital literacy skills.

2. Foster creativity-friendly school culture.

Build classroom environments that encourage experimentation and intellectual risk-taking. Teachers should use platforms such as podcasts, digital portfolios, or student-created videos to share diverse voices and innovative ideas, promoting curiosity and unique perspectives. Schools can host innovation showcases or hackathons where students share projects that reflect their backgrounds and interests to solve problems that are meaningful to them.

3. Develop personalized, flexible learning pathways.

Replace rigid, standardized education models with pathways tailored to individual talents and aspirations that resonate deeply with each learner. For example, students may engage with adaptive learning technologies, personalized AI-driven mentorship, or virtual collaborative projects to pursue passions in fields such as digital storytelling, STEM/STEAM innovation, social entrepreneurship, or creative arts.

4. Invest in innovation spaces and digital resources.

Create innovation hubs, maker spaces, or virtual creative studios equipped with modern technology—such as virtual reality, augmented reality, coding platforms, and media production tools. Providing these resources ensures marginalized students can access tools that support innovation and creative exploration, reducing digital inequities.

5. Build genuine partnerships for authentic learning.
Collaborate with local businesses, nonprofits, universities, and cultural organizations to provide meaningful real-world projects. These partnerships validate diverse pathways to success, helping students apply their creativity and innovation in real-world contexts.

6. Promote diverse student leadership and voice.
Empower marginalized students by giving them platforms to share their ideas, lead school projects, and shape their educational environment. Support youth-led podcasts, blogs, or digital media channels to share and amplify diverse experiences, fostering agency, belonging, and visibility.

Real inclusion means recognizing and cultivating the potential of every learner. Schools should replace uniform standards with flexible, personalized learning pathways, providing opportunities that genuinely match each student's passions, interests, and talents. This requires shifting from conformity-driven structures to environments where creativity flourishes as each person is recognized and celebrated. Assessment, likewise, must evolve to acknowledge innovation, effort, and originality, rather than mere conformity to standardized expectations.

True equity in education enables each student to meaningfully participate and contribute to the world. When schools center creativity, they dismantle barriers that disproportionately affect marginalized learners, especially students of color, those from lower socioeconomic backgrounds, learners with disabilities, or students whose talents have historically gone unrecognized. Prioritizing creativity creates environments where marginalized learners gain confidence, find their voices, and share unique perspectives that might otherwise remain hidden. Equity-driven creativity ensures that *all* students receive the freedom and resources to fully explore and express their potential. Every student deserves an education that intentionally cultivates their individual strengths and aspirations, removing the systemic barriers that perpetuate inequity.

18
Educating for a shared planet

We are living through overlapping global crises: climate breakdown, mass displacement, ecological collapse, rising authoritarianism, and digital fragmentation. They shape daily life. Young people are coming of age amid instability, inequality, and ecological fragility, yet most education systems still treat these conditions as peripheral or optional. Curricula remain siloed and inward-looking, disconnected from the realities students inhabit and the futures they must help shape.

If education is to remain relevant, it must shift from preparing students to succeed in a competitive marketplace to preparing them to sustain life on a shared planet. That is, we must remission education as a practice of shared responsibility, not as a means of individual advancement on its own. We need educational experiences that build students' capacities to understand interdependence, navigate complexity, and act with care across cultural and ecological boundaries. In short, we need to teach for *planetary citizenship* (OECD, 2020; Nussbaum, 2011).

Building a simple awareness of global problems will not contribute to solving these prblems; students must be prepared to respond with insight, care, and be ready to act with insight. We must shift from content delivery to a pedagogy rooted in relationships, systems thinking, and real-world engagement. Learning must help students make sense of complexity and act responsibly within it.

Global citizenship education pushes beyond textbook knowledge. It emphasizes empathy, ethical reasoning, and collaboration across difference. Rather than viewing global problems as distant, students are encouraged to connect them to their own communities and experiences. This approach moves away from a charity mindset. It centers solidarity, justice, and mutual learning, positioning students not as saviors, but as co-creators of sustainable futures.

From *Manifesto 25*:

> ***Acts of global citizenship transform personal experience into planetary impact.*** *Rooted in local contexts and meaningful engagement with diverse communities, it bridges individual perspectives with global challenges. Education must equip learners to tackle these challenges through cross-cultural empathy, ethical responsibility, and collaborative problem-solving. This requires planetary-focused literacies—frameworks that connect local actions to global solutions while respecting individual and collective rights. By aligning personal agency with shared tools, education empowers learners to act locally and globally, shaping sustainable and equitable futures.*

FROM GLOBAL TO PLANETARY CITIZENSHIP

Effective global citizenship education requires planetary-focused literacies, practical frameworks that help learners understand complex global dynamics and their relationship with local issues (Meadows, 2008). For example, students studying climate change might explore local impacts such as urban heat islands or agricultural disruptions, learning how community-specific actions can influence broader solutions. Through case studies and experiential projects, learners develop the capacity to analyze global systems and identify local leverage points for change.

Planetary citizenship extends the vision of global citizenship. This distinction matters because it shapes how we design learning: not only what we teach, but how we ask students to think, feel, and act. It recognizes that our responsibilities extend beyond people to the living systems that sustain us. Students learn to understand the Earth not just as a backdrop to human activity, but as a dynamic, interdependent system that demands care, humility, and action.

Table 2. Differentiating global citizenship from planetary citizenship.

CONCEPT	CORE FOCUS	KEY PRACTICES
Global citizenship	Civic participation and justice in a globalized world	Service learning, issue debates, human rights education
Planetary citizenship	Care, interdependence, and ecological sustainability	Systems thinking, local-global analysis, ethics-based action

To prepare students for life on a shared planet, education must:

- **Develop planetary literacies**: Frameworks that help learners connect local conditions to global systems and act with ecological and ethical insight.
- **Emphasize experiential learning**: Case studies, simulations, and community projects that expose learners to real-world complexities and dilemmas.
- **Foster cross-cultural empathy**: Opportunities to engage directly with diverse communities, challenge assumptions, and learn across difference.
- **Engage in ethical reasoning**: Teaching students to weigh competing responsibilities, between individual and collective, present and future, human and non-human.
- **Build collaborative skills**: Interdisciplinary teamwork that mirrors the interconnected nature of today's challenges.

Traditional education treats knowledge as static content. Planetary learning is dynamic, immersive, and relational. It asks students to absorb information *and* to reconsider their place in the world and their responsibility to it.

The EVOKE project, developed by the World Bank (2025, February 5) as a "crash course in changing the world," offers one illustration. Piloted in Africa and Latin America, EVOKE immerses learners in storytelling, game-based challenges, and real-world missions focused on food security, energy, water, and disaster resilience. Through role-play and systems thinking, students address local problems while drawing on global knowledge networks. The model positions learners not as future professionals-in-waiting, but as present agents capable of shaping outcomes with global relevance. It shows how narrative and play can cultivate empathy, innovation, and civic responsibility across contexts.

Learning to solve global grand challenges cultivates empathy, imagination, and agency. It bridges the gap between awareness and action, between local experience and planetary impact.

Developing planetary citizenship requires learning across difference. As students grapple with local-global issues, they must be equipped to listen, question assumptions, and engage with people whose perspectives may challenge their own. This demands intentional, proactive, and *preactive* strategies to bring the world into the classroom and the classroom into the world.

Internationalization plays a vital role in building planetary citizenship when it is grounded in equity and reciprocity. It is the intentional integration of global perspectives, cross-cultural engagement, and international collaboration into teaching, learning, and institutional practice. Done well, it moves beyond symbolic exchanges to prepare learners to navigate and contribute to an interconnected world. This requires embedding global perspectives deeply into curriculum and pedagogy, supported by meaningful partnerships, digital collaboration, and multilingual learning that foster empathy, cultural understanding, and shared responsibility for global challenges (Laesk, 2015).

To be meaningful, internationalization must go beyond superficial global themes or symbolic partnerships. It must integrate global perspectives into curriculum design, pedagogy, and institutional priorities, ensuring that learners engage with real-world issues from multiple cultural and geopolitical standpoints. When grounded in equity and reciprocity, internationalization can serve as a powerful driver of transformation, enabling students to connect personal agency with global impact.

This begins with empathy. Schools must create opportunities for learners to engage directly with diverse communities, whether through international partnerships, virtual exchanges, or community-based projects that cross cultural or socioeconomic boundaries. By fostering understanding and respect for different perspectives, learners become more capable collaborators, able to address global challenges collectively rather than in isolation.

Encouraging responsibility and agency equips learners to act decisively and with confidence. Education should help students understand their rights and duties within interconnected global systems, showing how personal interests connect to the well-being of others. Students build skills in reasoning and judgment, preparing them to address complex issues such as resource distribution, human rights, and environmental stewardship with care and effectiveness.

Collaborative problem-solving further enables learners to address global challenges practically. Schools should prioritize interdisciplinary projects, simulations, and problem-based learning experiences that require teamwork, negotiation, and the integration of diverse viewpoints. Such experiences teach students to manage complexities and uncertainties inherent in global issues, preparing them to craft sustainable and equitable solutions.

COURAGEOUS LEADERSHIP FOR A SHARED FUTURE

Equipping learners for a shared planetary future requires aligning individual agency with collective tools and responsibilities. Students need frameworks, relationships, and real-world experiences that help them translate local action into global impact. This shift will not happen on its own.

Courageous leadership is required to move beyond outdated metrics and short-term outcomes. It demands moral clarity and a willingness to act even when doing so is inconvenient or contested. Courageous leaders ask different questions. *What kind of world are we educating for? Who is missing from our vision of the future? What truths are we avoiding because they are difficult to teach?* They listen when students speak about fear, hope, and uncertainty. They respond by rethinking priorities, reallocating resources, and modeling responsibility.

This leadership is rarely dramatic. It appears in everyday choices: slowing a crowded curriculum to make space for reflection, challenging funding that undermines shared values, or inviting difficult conversations about equity and impact. It prioritizes trust over compliance and responsibility over convenience. Leaders understand that what is normalized in classrooms today defines what becomes possible tomorrow (see esp. Fullan, 2018; Senge, 2006).

Planetary citizenship will not emerge from revised lesson plans alone. It depends on how institutions are led and why. Courageous leadership creates the conditions for deeper learning, ethical clarity, and collective care. It signals to students that they are not being prepared to adapt to a broken world, but to repair and reimagine it.

The urgency is real. So is the possibility. If education responds with courage and conviction, it can help the next generation carry forward not only knowledge, but the capacity to build futures in which we may all flourish.

19
The future belongs to nerds, geeks, makers, dreamers, and *knowmads*

The future belongs to curious, passionate individuals unafraid to take intellectual risks, not to those who are passively obedient and skilled at following instructions. Social mobility is powered by creativity, innovation, and a willingness to embrace uncertainty, not compliance. Those best positioned for tomorrow are nerds, geeks, makers, dreamers, and knowmads: individuals skilled in navigating complexity, exploring new ideas, and translating knowledge into meaningful action.

From *Manifesto 25*:

> *The future belongs to nerds, geeks, makers, dreamers, and knowmads. While not everybody will or should become an entrepreneur, those who do not develop entrepreneurial skills are at a great disadvantage. Our education systems should focus on the development of **entreprenerds**: individuals who leverage their specialized knowledge to dream, create, make, explore, learn, and promote entrepreneurial, cultural, or social endeavors, taking risks and enjoying the process as much as the final outcome, without fearing the potential failures or mistakes that the journey includes.*

Knowmads are adaptable, creative individuals who learn, work, and innovate across diverse contexts, freely navigating disciplines, borders, and organizational structures. They leverage curiosity, resilience, and openness to uncertainty, shaping unique pathways through exploration and meaningful action.

Characteristics of knowmadic workers

Knowmads per Moravec (2013) are:

1. Are not restricted to a specific age;
2. Build their personal knowledge through explicit information gathering and tacit experiences, and leverage their personal knowledge to produce new ideas;
3. Are able to contextually apply their ideas and expertise in various social and organizational configurations;
4. Are highly motivated to collaborate, and are natural networkers, navigating new organizations, cultures, and societies;
5. Use new technologies purposively to help them solve problems and transcend limitations;
6. Are open to sharing what they know, and invite and support open access to information, knowledge, and expertise from others;
7. Can unlearn as quickly as they learn, adopting new ideas and practices as necessary;
8. Thrive in non-hierarchical networks and organizations;
9. Develop habits of mind and practice to learn continuously; and,
10. Are not afraid of failure.

Organizations increasingly require adaptive, diverse workers. In a world defined by rapid change, knowmadic workers navigate, adapt to, and create transformations effectively. Static roles rarely yield new value or innovation. Diverse perspectives combined with specialized expertise enable knowmads to lead, adapt, and thrive amid uncertainty.

Knowmads extend beyond formal organizations, present in every aspect of life. They differentiate between their jobs (specific employment roles) and their work, the personally meaningful activities they pursue long-term. Unlike linear careers defined externally, knowmadic work evolves through self-directed exploration. If opportunities for meaningful impact diminish, knowmads move forward, continuously redefining their professional and personal journeys.

The knowmadic mindset aligns naturally with the concept of *entreprenerds*. While knowmads thrive on adaptability and interdisciplinary exploration, entreprenerds specifically harness specialized knowledge and deep expertise to generate new value and outcomes. Both share entrepreneurial traits such as curiosity, resilience, and adaptability, but entreprenerds emphasize deep expertise as a foundation for bringing innovations to life.

Entrepreneurship involves more than starting businesses. It includes critical thinking, problem-solving, initiative, resilience, and adaptability—skills essential for success in a rapidly evolving world. While not everyone should become an entrepreneur (or would want to), those without these competencies risk falling behind, unprepared to navigate change or seize opportunities. Schools should therefore nurture entreprenerds, learners who combine specialized knowledge with an entrepreneurial mindset. Driven by curiosity and exploration, they embrace the journey as much as the final outcomes. They see mistakes as essential to growth, not setbacks. Entreprenerds experiment, iterate, and innovate continuously, actively shaping the future.

Schools must shift from standardized models that create predictable results to developing entrepreneurial qualities in students and new outcomes. Education should emphasize interdisciplinary learning, project-based tasks, and real-world challenges. Classrooms must encourage risk-taking and experimentation rather than punishing mistakes. Empowering students to innovate and collaborate helps them develop the confidence and skills to thrive in an unpredictable future.

Creating environments where entreprenerds thrive requires rethinking assessment practices. Schools should reward initiative, creativity, and resilience rather than conformity or memorization. Flexible curricula, student-led projects, and community partnerships provide authentic contexts for entrepreneurial skill development.

Five ways to cultivate entreprenerds in schools

1. **Interdisciplinary project-based learning**: Integrate knowledge across disciplines to design solutions for real community problems, fostering specialization and entrepreneurial initiative to solve grand challenges.

2. **Student-led innovation labs**: Create spaces where students experiment, prototype, and iterate, learning resilience and adaptability through hands-on exploration.

3. **Collaborative partnerships with local enterprises**: Engage students with local businesses, NGOs, and startups, applying academic and personal knowledge to real-world challenges while developing entrepreneurial skills.

4. **Failure-friendly assessments**: Design assessments that prioritize creative experimentation and meaningful effort over immediate success, normalizing risk-taking.

5. **Knowmadic experiences**: Offer internships, exchanges, or virtual collaborations across international borders and disciplines, building flexibility and innovation capacity.

Building a knowmad society requires transformative changes at personal, organizational, and policy levels. Educational institutions must shift away from rigid curricula toward flexible learning experiences that empower individuals to grow through exploration and discovery. Businesses must curate diverse teams that embrace uncertainty, cultivating an environment where innovation emerges naturally from collaboration and adaptability. Governments need to trust educators, invest thoughtfully, and support dynamic workforces through robust social policies. At an individual level, continuous self-assessment and lifelong learning become essential, allowing people to remain agile and ready for unforeseen opportunities.

Ultimately, fostering entreprenerds requires rethinking educational priorities and assessments. Rewarding creativity, initiative, and resilience enables students to practice entrepreneurial skills authentically. The future belongs not to those who fear failure but to those who find joy in exploring the unknown (Dweck, 2006; Kapur, 2016). Entreprenerds—nerds, geeks, makers, dreamers, and knowmads—will shape tomorrow, bringing individual-level, specialized knowledge and creative courage to overcome emerging challenges.

20
Reality is not optional

In the United States and elsewhere, we are witnessing a calculated retreat from empirical truth. Beyond mere rhetoric, the current shift toward dismantling government agencies—specifically those focused on public health, environmental science, and oversight—represents a structural attack on objective information. When the infrastructure for gathering data is defunded or dissolved, "facts" effectively cease to exist in the public record. This strategic silencing creates a vacuum where accountability vanishes, leaving society without the common ground required for critical thinking or collective action.

Manifesto 25 warns ignoring our shared reality invites chaos: without reliable information, society loses the common ground for critical thinking and collaboration. These sweeping measures erode public trust and threaten the empirical basis that education depends on, allowing distortions and evasions of accountability to flourish.

From *Manifesto 25*:

Reality is not optional. Ignoring our shared reality is a collapse into chaos. Weaponized postmodernism, where facts are twisted and account-

ability evaded, threatens the foundation of education and society itself. Shared realities are not optional; without them, critical thinking fails, trust evaporates, and collaboration becomes impossible. Education must confront distortion head-on, rooting itself in empirical evidence while unleashing our imaginations to solve new challenges. To build a sustainable future, learners must be equipped to challenge distortions, reject evasion of accountability, and navigate complexity with intellectual courage.

THE WAR ON REALITY

Reality is under attack on multiple fronts as orchestrated disinformation undermines public trust and warps our collective ability to understand or communicate (Vosoughi, Roy & Aral, 2018). The current administration in the United States (as of April 2026) has hurriedly dismantled or defunded essential agencies, interfering with data collection and research across fields ranging from public health to environmental science. This calculated, deliberate misrepresentation exemplifies weaponized postmodernism, where verifiable facts are twisted, essential truths are stripped of meaning, and accountability becomes impossible. The immediate consequence is a public left uncertain about which sources to trust, but the deeper casualty is the education system itself. Without reliable information and shared reference points, schools cannot cultivate informed, critically thinking learners, leaving society vulnerable to manipulation and control.

Weaponized postmodernism

Weaponized postmodernism is the deliberate distortion of facts and the erosion of shared reality to undermine critical thinking, dissolve accountability, and create a society more susceptible to manipulation by a power. While classical postmodernism questions absolute truths and examines the role of power in shaping knowledge, weaponized postmodernism exploits these ideas to push misinformation, discredit expertise, and blur the distinction between fact and fiction. By flooding public discourse with contradictory narratives and manufactured doubt, bad-faith actors can erode trust in institutions, making it easier to control public perception and suppress dissent. (Note. This definition is inspired by Lee McIntyre, 2018.)

When authoritarian movements seek to control society, one of their first battlegrounds is the education system. Disinformation campaigns target schools because eliminating critical thinking at an early stage weakens future resistance and ensures that propaganda can spread without challenge. This is an attack beyond knowledge—on societal stability itself. Once shared truth is eroded, polarization deepens, public trust collapses, and institutions fracture under the weight of competing realities. Chaos manifests as a society unable to solve problems, govern effectively, or unite around even the most basic facts; a society that relies on authoritarianism in perpetuity.

By casting doubt on empirical evidence, these campaigns discredit teachers, rewrite historical narratives, and suppress peer-reviewed consensus within classrooms. Students are left struggling to navigate contradictory claims, while educators face mounting hostility for upholding factual knowledge. In this climate of manufactured doubt, weaponized postmodernism takes hold: the dividing lines between facts, opinions, and blatant lies blur. Education's role in shaping informed, conscientious citizens collapses. By attacking both knowledge institutions and those who uphold them, disinformation erodes democracy and the very ability of a society to recognize reality itself.

Similar patterns emerge worldwide, where autocratic leaders exploit rapid disinformation campaigns to entrench power. By targeting and dismantling institutions responsible for gathering and disseminating factual information, these regimes eliminate scrutiny and foster echo chambers of distorted narratives. Democracies that rely on transparency and open dialogue cannot always respond quickly enough, and civic engagement unravels as a result. This breakdown in shared reality is further amplified by digital channels, undermining local governance and international coöperation on pressing issues such as climate change, global health, and economic stability. In this environment, education finds itself in a precarious position: without a factual baseline, schools cannot foster critical thinking or equip learners with the intellectual courage needed to navigate complexity. A society adrift in conspiracy and mistrust cannot effectively teach its youth, address urgent problems, coördinate global solutions, or unite around shared goals.

THE COMPLICITY OF BIG TECH

The rise of AI-generated propaganda has escalated this crisis even further, making traditional fact-checking methods insufficient. Deepfake videos, AI-generated news articles, and automated disinformation campaigns can now fabricate events, distort historical records, and manipulate public perception with alarming speed and emulated realism (UNESCO, 2025; World Economic Forum, 2024). Schools must evolve faster than these threats by teaching advanced media literacy and digital verification skills as a core competency, not an optional add-on. This means training students to analyze metadata, reverse-search images, recognize AI-generated patterns in text, and use skills and tools to verify sources. Without these skills, even the most critically minded learners risk being outpaced by technology designed to deceive. The education system can no longer rely on traditional methods of media analysis. The system must equip students to navigate a world where the line between reality and fabrication is increasingly difficult to discern, and one in which fabricated reality may be used against them.

Not long ago, the internet was seen as the great equalizer: a tool for democratizing knowledge, expanding access to education, and fostering global collaboration. But what was once heralded as a revolution for truth has been weaponized into an instrument of control. The very platforms that promised to unite the world are used to accelerate its fragmentation, flooding discourse with disinformation while silencing those who challenge it.

The disinformation crisis is engineered for profit. Social media platforms and Big Tech giants have designed systems that do not reward truth. They reward whatever keeps users engaged, whether that be conspiracy theories, extremist rhetoric, or AI-generated propaganda. The consequences of this extend far beyond individual misinformation. When falsehoods spread at algorithmic speed, reality itself fractures. Societies become locked in parallel, opposing versions of truth, making it impossible to engage in collective problem-solving. Climate change, public health crises, and even democracy itself become unsolvable problems when shared reality is replaced with AI-optimized delusions.

The crisis deepens when Big Tech leaders align themselves with authoritarian figures, shaping digital discourse to serve political agendas. As Trump and his allies consolidate power, many of Silicon Valley's most influential figures have abandoned even the pretense of neutrality, choosing instead to cater to political strongmen in exchange for deregulation, tax breaks, and influence. Social media platforms have long demonstrated selective enforcement of policies, for example, allowing misinformation and propaganda from those in power to spread unchecked. This is a betrayal of the fundamental role technology was supposed to play in an open society. But if the internet was once a tool for knowledge and collaboration, it can be reclaimed as one again … if we take decisive action.

SCHOOLS ARE THE FRONTLINES OF TRUTH

Education must stand at the forefront of countering systematic distortions because it shapes the foundational skills and values young minds carry into adulthood. Schools impart facts, but they also prepare students to navigate a rapidly changing world. When educators ignore or downplay disinformation, they fail in their responsibility to cultivate informed, reflective citizens. A society that does not equip its youth to discern truth from manipulation risks losing its ability to confront future challenges with clarity and unity. A strong curriculum relies on quality information backed by verifiable, empirical evidence. Science, mathematics (especially statistics), and the humanities provide opportunities for students to practice critical thinking and distinguish credible sources from misinformation. Yet academic content alone is not enough. Students must also develop an ethical framework that helps them understand the real-world consequences of spreading falsehoods.

This is especially urgent in a world where official channels can perpetuate misleading narratives. Learning to differentiate between valid expertise and unsubstantiated claims, whether from social media influencers, corporate PR campaigns, or political leaders, is a vital civic skill. Structured debates, research projects, and collaborative problem-solving teach learners to analyze arguments, cross-check sources, and refine their perspectives based on evidence. But formal instruction is only part of the solution. Free play (open-ended, unstructured exploration) encourages curiosity, adaptability, and the confidence to question assumptions. When students engage in unscripted problem-solving, experimentation, and creative expression, they develop the cognitive flexibility necessary to challenge disinformation and think independently. Classrooms should serve as incubators for reasoned inquiry, where students are encouraged to ask difficult questions, evaluate diverse viewpoints, and adjust their thinking in response to new information. By fostering intellectual curiosity and resilience, education becomes a powerful defense against manipulation and a foundation for democratic engagement.

To build a sustainable future, learners need far more than rote knowledge of facts or theories; they need the fortitude to question authority in a constructive way and the resolve to maintain intellectual integrity in the face of distorted realities. An educational environment that values intellectual courage encourages students to weigh the merits of competing ideas rather than accepting them at face value. Through exposure to conflicting points of view and guidance on how to judge them critically, schools foster the habits of curiosity, discernment, and empathy necessary for global problem-solving. In embracing this responsibility, education defends reality from those who would deny it, and also empowers the next generation to uphold truth, promote accountability, and chart a course toward a more equitable and informed society.

SIX WAYS TO PROTECT TRUTH THROUGH A POSITIVE REBELLION

Schools often face strict guidelines and limited autonomy, making it challenging to counter disinformation openly. Nonetheless, educators, parents, and students can engage in acts of positive rebellion: small but meaningful efforts to maintain shared realities and bolster critical thought, even under restrictive conditions.

POSTIVE REBELLION

> ***Positive rebellion*** *is the act of resisting misinformation, censorship, and ideological distortions in education through ethical, strategic, and collective action. It does not seek chaos or defiance for its own sake but instead upholds truth, critical thinking, and academic integrity against political manipulation. Positive rebellion can take many forms: sharing fact-based resources, forming coalitions to protect evidence-based curricula, challenging disinformation in public forums, or creating alternative educational spaces when formal institutions fail. It is a commitment to defending reality, not through force, but through knowledge, collaboration, and unwavering intellectual courage.*

Given the gravity of the threat, here are actions educators and communities can take meaningful steps within even the most restrictive environments:

1. Build coalitions within the system to safeguard truth.

In restrictive environments, educators need one another to keep reality visible. This work begins with small, careful networks that share reliable materials, compare lesson plans, and help students reach knowledge placed out of view. Teachers meet after hours, trade reading lists, and create parallel spaces where evidence still matters. These efforts do not look heroic from the outside. They look like colleagues protecting one another and protecting their students. Yet they keep facts alive when institutions try to push them aside.

2. Leverage student curiosity and initiative as defenders of fact-based learning

Students are not passive recipients of education. They are the most direct stakeholders in the struggle for truth. Schools should support student-led organizations that investigate misinformation, challenge curriculum distortions, and demand transparency from administrators. High school students can document censorship efforts, expose politically motivated curriculum changes, and use social media to spread fact-based resources. This movement must go beyond small discussion clubs and should be a coördinated effort to resist educational disinformation at its source.

3. Build community hubs and partnerships.

When formal education is compromised, external institutions must step in. Libraries, universities, nonprofits, and independent learning spaces can provide fact-based learning through workshops, public lectures, and open-access resources. As government research agencies are dismantled, universities must take on a greater role in preserving and sharing credible knowledge. Schools can discreetly connect students and families to these trusted sources, ensuring communities remain informed even when official channels fail. This exchange must flow both ways: universities can act as knowledge curators and guardians, while local schools become knowledge diffusers. Schools can integrate university research into their curricula and distribute reliable scientific findings through their activities. Likewise, universities should establish rapid-response networks to meet schools' emerging issues, ensuring students have direct access to experts rather than relying on politicized media narratives. By fostering this reciprocal relationship, universities and schools together create a decentralized, community-driven defense against disinformation.

4. Embed critical thinking and media literacy integration across the curriculum.

Media literacy cannot be an isolated elective that can be easily cut or politicized. It must be woven into all subjects. History should analyze propaganda and revisionism. Science must emphasize the difference between peer-reviewed research and pseudoscience. Mathematics should teach statistical manipulation and data bias. When fact-checking and critical analysis become integrated across disciplines, students develop instinctive resistance to misinformation rather than seeing it as an abstract skill.

5. Model intellectual courage and accountability.

Educators must set the standard for intellectual courage by refusing to treat falsehoods as equal to facts. This does necessarily suggest displays of open defiance. It can be as subtle as challenging misleading statements, reinforcing the importance of academic integrity, and using Socratic questioning to lead students toward truth. Where possible, educators should publicly document censorship attempts, advocate for policies that protect evidence-based curricula, and create safe spaces where students can critically engage with real information. Even in restrictive environments, demonstrating unwavering commitment to truth sends a powerful message: education serves reality, not political convenience.

6. Lead a positive rebellion against the politicization of education.
Disinformation thrives when opposition is disorganized and silent. Educators, students, and parents must act collectively to push back against politically motivated distortions. This means confronting school boards, exposing ideological curriculum interference, and leveraging media coverage to force accountability. Resistance should escalate when necessary, e.g., through lawsuits against censorship policies, teacher strikes, student walkouts, and the creation of independent education networks that operate beyond state influence. If public education is weaponized to serve ideology, our focus must shift toward reclaiming and rebuilding it.

The fight for truth in education must be focused on defending the future. When disinformation infiltrates schools, educators and students are not simply victims of manipulation; they are the last line of defense. To remain silent in the face of political distortions is to surrender reality itself.

By practicing these forms of constructive defiance, schools can resist the spread of weaponized postmodernism from within. The goal is not to break rules or create spectacle, but to uphold the principle that reality must remain the foundation of any meaningful education. Over time, these efforts can shift institutional culture toward one that honors evidence, nurtures critical thinking, and protects our collective sense of what is real, even in an era of widespread disinformation.

IF SCHOOLS FAIL, COMMUNITIES MUST STEP IN

If the public education system continues to be undermined and trust in formal institutions erodes beyond repair, communities may have no choice but to organize education outside of the traditional system. While this may seem like conceding defeat, it is, in reality, an act of resistance. It ensures truth, critical thinking, and evidence-based learning do not disappear entirely. Community-led education initiatives, independent learning coöperatives, and non-formal, decentralized networks of educators can step in where public schools are weakened, providing students with access to reliable knowledge and intellectual growth free from political interference. Libraries, local organizations, and even digital platforms can serve as alternative learning hubs, creating parallel structures that safeguard fact-based education.

However, we must acknowledge fully replacing public education risks furthering a hostile administration's goal of eroding trust in shared institutions, so this approach should be a last resort rather than an immediate alternative. The priority must remain fighting for the integrity of the existing system, pressuring local governments, mobilizing educators, and advocating for policies that reinforce the role of education in democracy. But if traditional schools become wholly ineffective or compromised, communities of educators and learners must be prepared to step in and reclaim education for themselves, ensuring that future generations still have the tools to seek truth, think critically, and hold power accountable.

RECLAIMING DIGITAL SPACES FOR TRUTH

The rebellion against disinformation is happening online, in real time. Students spend hours consuming social media, engaging with content curated by algorithms that reward sensationalism over accuracy. The internet was built on the promise of knowledge-sharing. If it has been weaponized, it must be reclaimed. And there is little time left. AI-generated propaganda is advancing at an unprecedented pace. Soon, entire news events, video footage, and historical records will be indistinguishable from truth (Guan, Horan & Zhan, 2025). This means that students must learn to recognize digital deception and actively push back against it. Without this ability, we risk a future where no one can verify what is real, making truth itself irrelevant.

Educators and students must take an active role in shaping digital spaces into forums for truth rather than platforms for deception. This requires a shift in how we approach media literacy, not as a passive defense, but as an offensive strategy. Schools must move beyond teaching students to identify fake news and instead train them to confront disinformation where it spreads, disrupt harmful narratives, and become digital first responders for truth.

Educators can integrate real-world fact-checking exercises into assignments, encouraging students to investigate viral claims, analyze manipulated media, and publish their findings. Student-led fact-checking teams, modeled after investigative journalism, can train learners to use reverse image searches, AI-detection tools, and data verification techniques, arming them with the skills necessary to push back against fabricated content.

Schools should also embrace counter-disinformation campaigns as part of project-based learning. Instead of simply consuming and critiquing information, students should be empowered to produce and circulate fact-based content, whether through blogs, social media posts, or video explainers that debunk myths in real time. By leveraging their own digital fluency, students can become active participants in the fight for reality rather than passive consumers of algorithm-driven misinformation.

Perhaps most importantly, educators must create safe spaces for digital activism. Students who challenge misinformation often face backlash, harassment, and attempts to silence them. Schools should provide structured spaces for digital resilience, ethical responsibility, and the psychological toll of online disinformation battles. Just as activists are trained in civil resistance, students must be trained to navigate digital spaces with both courage and strategy.

THE FIGHT FOR EDUCATION IS A FIGHT FOR DEMOCRACY

Sudden shifts toward authoritarian power are stark reminders that political forces can overturn what once seemed stable. Facts can become casualties in power struggles, and entire societies can be trapped in cycles of misinformation. Human decency and democratic principles require us to address these threats without resorting to the same manipulative tactics. Instead, we must reaffirm that shared reality underpins all meaningful progress.

Defending schools from disinformation is not enough. If education remains reactive, countering falsehoods as they appear, then the cycle of manipulation will continue. The real challenge is not centered only on fighting propaganda but ensuring that the education system itself is designed to be resistant to it in the first place. This requires rethinking how we teach truth, build resilience against misinformation, and structure learning environments that cannot be easily co-opted by political agendas.

A truly propaganda-resistant education system must must equip learners with the intellectual self-defense necessary to recognize manipulation before it takes hold. This means prioritizing metacognitive and epistemic education (i.e., knowing what we do not know and how we know what we know) alongside traditional subjects; not just teaching "the facts." It means embedding media literacy and cognitive bias training at every level of schooling, not as an afterthought, but as a core component of every discipline. It requires teacher autonomy to challenge disinformation without fear of political retaliation, robust protections for academic integrity, and educational policies that safeguard curricula from ideological interference.

Without these systemic changes, education will always be vulnerable to the next wave of disinformation. The goal should not be limited to resisting propaganda but to create generations of learners who are fundamentally immune to it.

Education has always shaped the future, but never before has it determined whether the future itself remains grounded in reality. There is no longer a question of what students should learn. The question is whether truth will continue to exist in the public sphere at all. If we allow disinformation to take root in classrooms, we surrender the ability to solve global challenges, defend human rights, and protect democratic governance.

Educators, policymakers, and civil society at large have a duty to protect and strengthen that shared reality. We must insist on verifiable truth as the cornerstone of knowledge, even when faced with organized campaigns to discredit it. If we ignore reality, the alternative is chaos.

21
The missing planet

A school day begins with a familiar rhythm. Students move from worksheets to whiteboards while forests burn and rivers shrink outside. Children memorize the parts of a leaf while the trees that once bore them vanish. School routines continue, unaware (or unwilling to acknowledge) that the world beyond the classroom is unraveling.

Modern education still mirrors the industrial systems that helped produce this crisis: extractive, hierarchical, and standardized. Schools prepare students for the world that caused collapse, not for the one that must emerge after it.

From *Manifesto 25*:

> *An education that ignores the planet is an education without a future. With climate catastrophe looming, any curriculum that neglects environmental stewardship is both deficient and irresponsible. Education must actively shape students' futures and the world around them. Learners should not passively study the environment; they must be empowered as co-creators of solutions and active guardians of the planet. By enabling students with future-ready skills and agency to address grand challenges, and integrating planetary-focused literacies into a dynamic, flexible learning process, we foster innovation and a personal connection to sustainability that inspires lasting impact.*

Climate collapse is the defining reality of our time, globally (IPCC, 2023). The task before us is to reinvent education so that sustainability and care for the planet are not side lessons, but foundations for how we learn, teach, and live.

Stewardship (taking care of the planet) is a good starting point, but we must go further. The Earth will continue for billions of years, but human life on it will not ...*unless we change course.*

Today's learners must be empowered to address the causes of the crisis, moving beyond adaptation. This calls for an education that sees them not as future workers or consumers, but as planetary citizens, individuals with the insight, agency, and responsibility to help shape a livable future.

EDUCATING BEYOND CLIMATE AWARENESS

Schools have taught environmental content for decades. Posters outline the water cycle. Earth Day is celebrated once a year. Students sort recycling or build solar ovens. Too often, education stops at awareness. Problems are named without pathways for action. Consequences are described without tools for response. The result is familiarity without power: students who understand the crisis but feel unable to influence it.

Stewardship begins where awareness ends. It emerges when learners are invited to participate in—*and shape*—the world. Real empowerment means students see themselves as agents of change, not passive recipients of information. This is where agency and self-efficacy converge (Bandura, 1997). Agency offers real choice. Self-efficacy provides the confidence that those choices matter. When learning connects directly to lived challenges, education becomes a purposeful response to the world.

Youth-led sustainability councils provide one example. In many cities, students audit school energy use, redesign waste systems, and present proposals to administrators and local officials. Where councils hold defined authority, their recommendations have influenced budgets and operating practices. These students do more than rehearse civic participation by linking analysis with action and reflection. This is *praxis.*

Community mapping projects offer another model. Learners document air quality, food access, or green space in their neighborhoods using open tools and guided inquiry. In producing data that did not previously exist, students locate themselves within living systems and recognize their capacity to influence them. Many of the most impactful efforts occur outside the formal classroom. Environmental clubs partner with local farms. Teenagers design apps for tracking bird migration. Young people organize climate teach-ins or public art projects to inspire change. These informal and nonformal spaces often do more to foster environmental responsibility than any textbook unit ever could. They thrive because they are learner-driven, connected to place, and rooted in care.

Empowerment is a practice. When education supports students in acting meaningfully within their communities, it builds lasting habits of engagement. And as those habits grow, so does the capacity to think beyond the individual and act on behalf of the collective, the future, and the planet itself.

PLANETARY LITERACIES FOR A LIVABLE FUTURE

To respond meaningfully to an emergent ecological collapse, learners need more than sets of information; they need new ways of perceiving, imagining, and participating. Planetary literacies offer a foundation for understanding complexity, anticipating change, and shaping more livable futures with care and clarity. These are not subjects to be added to the curriculum, but lenses that reframe how all learning happens.

Three core literacies help learners navigate this moment: ecological literacy, futures literacy, and systems thinking (OECD, 2018).

1. Ecological literacy

Ecological literacy grounds learning in the patterns of the living world. It invites students to explore interdependence, resilience, biodiversity, and limits as conditions of life. Ecologically literate learners understand how water cycles through a watershed, how forests regulate climate, and how waste becomes nourishment in healthy ecosystems. This literacy cultivates reverence alongside knowledge. It teaches that humans are not separate from nature but embedded within it.

2. Futures literacy

Futures literacy, as promoted by UNESCO (2019), builds the capacity to imagine and prepare for many possible futures. It trains learners to question assumptions, anticipate consequences, and expand their sense of what's possible. The goal is to develop strategies for exploring alternatives and navigating uncertainty with creativity. Futures-literate students don't ask, "What will happen to us?" They ask, "What could we do to help form preferred futures, together?"

3. Systems thinking

Systems thinking helps learners perceive the loops, layers, and feedback dynamics of complex systems, whether ecological, social, or technological. It teaches that problems are rarely linear, that causes and consequences are often distant in time and space, and that change in one part of a system can ripple through the whole. With this literacy, students learn to connect dots across disciplines and scales, to see patterns, and to design more thoughtful interventions.

These literacies are already echoed in global frameworks. The OECD's (2018) *Future of Education and Skills 2030* project emphasizes systems thinking and anticipation as key competencies for navigating complexity. UNESCO's (2021) *Reimagining our Futures Together* report urges schools to prepare learners for ecological transformation and civic imagination. *Manifesto 25* calls for "future-ready skills" that blend personal agency with collective responsibility, a broader expression of planetary literacies.

What unites these approaches is perspective over content. A math class might model climate feedback loops. A literature seminar might explore speculative fiction as a tool for imagining different futures. A history unit might trace how industrial energy systems shaped modern inequality. Across subjects, planetary literacies connect learning to life.

To learn for a livable future, education must nurture minds that can think across boundaries, imagine beyond crisis, and act with care in a fragile, interdependent world.

REGENERATIVE PEDAGOGIES

We cannot teach for a living planet with dead pedagogies. If we are to prepare learners to live well in an age of ecological uncertainty, we must also transform how learning happens. Regenerative education requires pedagogies that are attuned to place, culture, and complexity. It demands a shift from rigid delivery to dynamic participation, from abstraction to connection, and from fragmentation to wholeness.

First, we must move beyond curriculum silos. The climate crisis does not respect academic departments, and neither should our approach to learning. Regenerative pedagogies embrace integrated, interdisciplinary learning that mirrors the complexity of real-world challenges. A single project (e.g., restoring a local wetland) can draw on biology, ethics, data analysis, storytelling, and civics. Students don't merely learn about systems. They learn within them.

Second, we must reconnect education to place. For many learners, school has become an entirely indoor affair: disconnected from the seasons, shielded from the weather, and insulated from the land. Regenerative learning invites learners outside—into forests, rivers, gardens, and communities. Forest schools immerse children in ecological cycles. Indigenous-led land-based education, grounded in relational worldviews, teaches learners to listen, observe, and act in ways that honor interdependence and responsibility. Even where access to nature is limited, virtual visits to ecologically vulnerable areas (such as disappearing coastlines or fragile coral reefs) can help cultivate emotional and cognitive connection across distance.

Third, we must shift from performance to participation. In conventional classrooms, students are often tasked with repeating knowledge to prove they've learned. In contrast, regenerative pedagogies invite them to participate in knowledge creation, i.e., to ask questions, propose solutions, test ideas, and reflect on the outcomes. It's the difference between writing a paper on climate change and organizing a local campaign to reduce waste. Participation turns learning into lived experience (Scardamalia & Bereiter, 2010).

We see this in models such as:

- **Forest schools** (originating in Scandinavia) that center nature as both setting and teacher, nurturing resilience, curiosity, and ecological connection.
- **Indigenous-led land learning**, such as those practiced by Māori and First Nations educators (Stucki, 2010; Chief, 2017), that embed ancestral wisdom and stewardship in every lesson.
- **Teach the Future**, a global movement empowering youth to integrate climate futures into every subject, not as a niche topic but as an ethical imperative.
- **Green School Bali**, where sustainability is a way of life, from bamboo classrooms to community partnerships and renewable energy systems.

Technology, too, has a role to play, but only when used with *purpose*. Interactive simulations, real-time environmental data dashboards, and global collaboration platforms can support ecological learning when they connect learners meaningfully to each other and to the world.

Teaching for the planet requires more than awareness campaigns or science units on climate. It calls for a whole-pedagogy approach: one that regenerates our connection to land, to each other, and to the future. This prepares learners to think differently, across scales, across disciplines, and across generations.

RECLAIMING EDUCATION FOR THE EARTH

If the industrial age turned education into a mechanism for managing resources (human and ecological alike) the coming era must reclaim it as a force for regeneration. Education cannot remain an instrument of the very systems that eroded the planet's resilience. It must become a living, adaptive practice that helps us repair, restore, and reimagine our relationship with the Earth.

This means more than teaching about sustainability. It requires rethinking *what* education is for and *for whom* it is designed to benefit.

A regenerative education asks: *What kind of world are we preparing learners to inherit and co-create?* It sees every lesson as a potential act of healing. When students plant trees, test soil, restore native species, and listen to elders share stories of a place before it was paved over, they become caretakers. When they imagine better futures and organize for change, they embody the possibility that learning can make things whole again.

This is about survival. And it is already happening in bits and pieces that add up toward making a difference: schools that compost their food waste, in classrooms that transform stormwater into gardens, and in youth organizing themselves to demand climate action. These are small-scale practices with deep cultural implications: they teach learners that their actions matter, that interconnection is real, and that education has the power to regenerate life, not extract from it.

But to scale this shift, we must confront a deeper challenge: *How do we design learning environments that heal rather than harm, resisting the extractive logics of testing and ranking while supporting restoration, reflection, and responsibility? How do we place local ecologies, ancestral knowledge, and lived experience at the heart of the curriculum?*

The work begins with vision. A commitment to aligning daily educational practice with the living systems that sustain us. A decision to treat learners as planetary citizens. A belief that schools can be places where our relationship with the Earth is repaired.

EDUCATION MUST HELP US LIVE BETTER WITH THE EARTH OR IT WILL HAVE FAILED ITS PURPOSE ENTIRELY.

CAHIER FOUR

Systemic forces and barriers

FRAMING

*Education stands at a crossroads. Around the world, inequities persist, leaving entire communities unheard and underserved. Any system that accepts this status quo is complicit in injustice. To move forward, education must dismantle the barriers that exclude learners and build curricula that center the experiences, knowledge, and voices of those historically pushed aside. **Equity and inclusion are the foundation of a just education system.***

But equity cannot stand alone. Learners must also be prepared to act as citizens of both their local contexts and the wider planet. Global citizenship links personal experience to planetary challenges, demanding empathy across cultures and collective responsibility for the future we share. This requires more than abstract ideals: education must provide the literacies and tools that allow learners to connect what they do locally with how it shapes the global community.

To thrive in this context, students need spaces where imagination and initiative are valued. The future belongs to those who create, tinker, and take risks: nerds, geeks, makers, dreamers, and knowmads. Education must embrace entreprenerds: learners who transform specialized knowledge into ventures that carry cultural, social, and entrepreneurial value. Failure is not an endpoint but part of the process of learning, inventing, and reshaping the world.

At the same time, education must hold firm against distortion. We experience a shared reality. Without shared truths, critical thinking collapses, trust erodes, and coöperation fails. Learners must be prepared to navigate a world where facts are contested and misinformation spreads, balancing empirical evidence with the courage to imagine new possibilities. Education must defend reality while equipping learners to question, test, and build knowledge.

Finally, education that ignores the planet ignores the future itself. With climate change and ecological collapse looming, environmental stewardship can no longer be treated as an elective concern. Learners should not only study sustainability; they must be empowered as co-creators of solutions, with skills to act and innovate. This is the work of preparing for survival and flourishing in a changing world.

Taken together, these commitments (equity, global citizenship, entreprenerds, shared reality, and planetary stewardship) are interwoven strands of the same challenge. Education must reimagine itself as the ground where justice, truth, creativity, and sustainability converge. Anything less risks irrelevance in the face of the future that is already arriving.

PROMPTS FOR REFLECTION

1. **Complicity or change.** Where in your own context do you see inequities being tolerated or excused? What would dismantling them require, and where would you find points of resistance?
2. **Local to global.** How do your everyday choices, as a learner or educator, ripple into global challenges? Where do you see the gap between rhetoric and responsibility?
3. **Entreprenerds.** Where are learners in your world allowed to take risks, fail, and try again, and where are they punished into conformity? What spaces would unleash genuine creativity and initiative?

4. **Shared reality.** How do you navigate misinformation, distortion, or denial in your learning environment? What practices help defend truth while still leaving room for imagination?

5. **Planetary futures.** What would it take for your school, university, or workplace to embed sustainability as a lived practice, not an elective? What would have to be abandoned to make space for it?

Try this

Pull out a sheet of paper or use the notes pages that follow. Identify one inequity in your learning environment. Draft a concrete disruption: a reallocation of resources, a curriculum change, or a partnership that directly challenges the inequity. Commit to testing it within the next three months.

Notes

Notes

Notes

INTER MEZZO
2

CONSTRUIR
UNA
REBELIÓN
POSITIVA

BREAKING AWAY, REDEFINING FREEDOM

When we wrote *Manifesto 25*, we knew it would never be complete. It was never meant to be a prescription or a closed doctrine, but an open provocation—an invitation to question, revise, and expand what education could become. The manifesto asked readers not for agreement, but for critical responses.

The original signatories of the manifesto were invited to respond to two questions:

1. What practices or habits are you breaking away from, and why? Which educational assumptions do you now recognize as myths or traps?
2. Where do you see learning freedom struggling, thriving, or being redefined—in your professional, geographic, or political context?

Educators, activists, learners, and community builders from around the world answered. Their contexts differed, but their purpose converged: to rethink how we understand and practice learning. What follows is a synthesis of those reflections, a pause between the manifesto's provocations, and an opportunity to listen across boundaries.

The first observation is cultural. We inherit more than physical traits from earlier generations. We inherit beliefs, rituals, and habits so ingrained they become invisible. These traditions shape how we think about learning, school, and education itself. Some help us grow. Others trap us in outdated patterns until someone decides to step aside and question them.

Constanze Beyer captures this tension with a metaphor:

AI SITS IN A BOX AND PROCESSES TEXTS AND IMAGES ABOUT THE WORLD OUTSIDE. STUDENTS SIT IN BOXES AND PROCESS TEXTS AND IMAGES ABOUT THE WORLD OUTSIDE.

The difference, she explains, is that students can leave "the box." They can explore, connect, and experience. That potential is squandered when classrooms and curricula cut them off from the real world.

Let's give students the freedom to explore the world outside the classroom, to interact with people, to make mistakes and learn from them, to coöperate with others instead of competing.

Yet the box is no longer only physical. **Bob Kartous** reminds us it is also digital. Algorithms shape attention, manipulate emotion, and trap learners in echo chambers designed for profit rather than growth. Learning freedom today requires not only the ability to leave the classroom box, but the capacity to navigate the digital jungle with discernment, resilience, and care.

THE BOX HAS MANY FORMS

This box is not always made of four physical walls. **Minh Trung Doan**, reflecting from Vietnam, sees it reinforced in policies and practices that rush to embrace novelty without preparing the ground for it. "Shiny tech tools enter classrooms with great fanfare, but they often lack the emotional and social scaffolding necessary for inclusive learning."

He points out that "spaces for non-formal learning, homeschooling, and creative alternatives are either marginalized or dismissed altogether." In his view, even within formal systems, too many models remain outdated, offering learning environments that are neither culturally responsive nor attuned to the complexities of a hyperconnected world.

For him, the most glaring absence is planetary awareness. Despite the urgency voiced by scientists and climate movements, ecological literacy is still peripheral. Education has not caught up with the planetary consciousness that current and future generations need. Yet he also sees hope in the activism of young people. Armed with intersectional awareness and creative advocacy, they are not waiting for systems to reform. They are building community education hubs, challenging digital divides, and inventing new forms of solidarity that redesign education from below.

The redefinition of learning freedom, he argues, is happening elsewhere: "in living rooms, public squares, digital networks, and informal gatherings — anywhere curiosity resists containment." This involves transforming our entire idea of what learning should be: "dynamic, inclusive, joyful, sustainable, and empowering."

BREAKING THE RACETRACK MENTALITY

Curiosity, however, is hard to sustain in a culture that treats education as a race. **Alejandra Mendoza Garza** has seen the pattern repeatedly: "Whether it's 'getting to the weekend,' 'getting to the end of the semester,' or 'getting to the end of the year,' we are always running."

This "race," she argues, is an exhausting myth that leaves students, teachers, and leaders burned out. Education becomes about getting to a finish line rather than experiencing. She describes the toll of rigid timelines, heavy workloads, and leadership cultures that normalize constant motion: "When teachers run, leaders run, and parents run, we inevitably make our students run too, and we all end up tired."

Her alternative is to "deconstruct the idea of the race" and focus on the journey, where goals are "opportunities for learning… not just checkpoints." Learning, she reminds us, occurs in ecosystems, not in boxes or hamster wheels.

She further warns against fear-driven responses to technology, particularly AI. To ban or restrict AI without exploring its potential is, she argues, another form of running away. Like past moral panics over television or home computers, it reflects fear more than ethics. "Nothing in life is to be feared; it is only to be understood," she recalls from Marie Curie. For Alejandra, rejecting AI is a trap: the challenge is to teach the ethics and creativity needed to use it responsibly.

Drawing on Robert Merton's (1938) framework of deviant adaptations (conformity, innovation, ritualism, retreatism, rebellion), she sees learning freedom provoking a range of responses from conformity to rebellion. For her, disruption is a necessary stance in contexts where education is misused as political spectacle.

She also points to how political agendas can turn education into a "showcase," where programs are launched for visibility and votes but abandoned before they take root. In these contexts, she sees disruption not as a slogan but as a necessity: a conscious refusal of superficial reforms in favor of deeper, slower, more human transformations.

FINDING NEW PURPOSE

Shifting pace is one step; shifting purpose is another. **Silvia Enríquez** warns of the trap of mismatched intentions and methods. She has spent years teaching linguistics and educational technology to trainee teachers, pushing them to apply theory to their own practice. She tells students explicitly why they are studying theory and asks them to reflect on its value for their own work, rather than treating it as abstract content to be memorized.

Yet this approach often collides with the reality of exams, which create a state of contradictions that undermine innovative teaching:

If you try to teach your students to think… but then you have to use an exam format that is just repetition… then what's the point of having taught differently?

For her, change must be holistic: curriculum, assessment, and classroom culture moving in the same direction. Otherwise, students revert to what they know, studying to jump through hoops necessary to pass the course, rather than studying to learn.

Silvia also highlights collaboration as an antidote to the trap of repetition. In her classes, trainee teachers are asked to solve problems together, each contributing from their own practice. coöperation does not come easily in systems that reward individual performance, but she insists it must be practiced deliberately. When students experience the value of collaborative problem-solving, they are more likely to reproduce it in their own classrooms. For her, the point is clear: change cannot stop with new methods alone. It must reach curriculum, assessment, and culture at once.

INTEGRATION INSTEAD OF FRAGMENTATION

For **Luis R. Lara**, the break with tradition involves integration. Teaching electronics, he refuses to treat his subject as a self-contained silo:

Our education has historically been delivered in a fragmented way… But why not do it at the very same moment we are learning…?

He argues that real-world problems are inherently multidisciplinary, involving social, ecological, and economic considerations, alongside communication, marketing, and environmental care. Waiting until professional life to integrate these perspectives is a missed opportunity. If students learn in context from the beginning, they can become professionals who act in harmony with their environment and community.

Richard Fransham reinforces this integrative perspective through age-mixing. Drawing from a Canadian pilot program, he tells the story of two older students who entered intending to isolate themselves but soon realized that age differences dissolved when they worked in a mixed community. What began as separation turned into solidarity, showing that age segregation, like disciplinary fragmentation, impoverishes learning. Integration (across subjects and across generations) creates the conditions for empathy, resilience, and shared growth. The boys even admitted they had intended to ignore the younger students, but soon realized that prejudice dissolved in practice. The community taught them that age barriers are artificial.

REJECTING STANDARDIZATION

The **Cloud School** team in Poland challenges other myths: the belief that education must be "linear, standardized, and equal for everyone" and the reliance on grading and ranking as motivators. They see how "numbers can kill natural curiosity and motivation to learn."

Their critique resonates with **Christel Hartkamp's** reflections on the Sudbury model. She describes how schools that trust children to direct their own learning dismantle two of the most enduring myths: that children require constant external motivation, and that learning must be measured to count. In practice, Sudbury students choose their paths, engage across ages, and learn democratically. For Hartkamp, breaking with convention facilitates reclaiming faith in human potential.

Instead, they use "feedback, dialogue, and self-reflection" and focus on questions such as "What have we learned? What can we improve? What have we achieved?" They define the freedom to learn as "the right to choose, the right to make mistakes, and the right to set goals independently."

They acknowledge that systemic limitations (e.g., overloaded curricula, bureaucracy, and external control) still hold back bolder experimentation. But they also see freedom flourishing in self-learning groups, mentoring sessions, and student initiatives. Technology and remote models dissolve geographical barriers, allowing young people from around the world to collaborate and co-create.

PLACING TRUST IN LEARNERS

Trust is also central to Christel Hartkamp's engagement with the Sudbury model. She describes its premise:

Rather than seeing education as a passive act of receiving knowledge, Sudbury schools view it as an active, self-driven exploration.

In Sudbury-type schools, there are no grades, no mandatory classes, and no top-down curriculum. There is only trust that children are naturally curious and capable of directing their own learning. The model challenges two pervasive assumptions: that children require constant external motivation, and that learning must be measured and ranked to count.

Breaking free, she says, is "an act of reclaiming our faith in human potential."

EDUCATION AS A RIGHTS ISSUE

For **Juraj Mazák**, this is a matter of rights. "One of the biggest lies... is that education is something done to children." Children, he insists, are "rights-holders" entitled to an education that respects their autonomy and potential.

Grades, standardization, and micro-managed curricula are, in his words, mechanisms of exclusion. He argues that "deregulation isn't chaos—it's primarily a possibility. It's air." Without it, schools cannot adapt, care, include, or imagine better futures.

He rejects three myths in particular: that control creates quality, that standardization ensures fairness, and that school is only preparation for life. Each, he argues, betrays children's rights.

He challenges us:

If we truly want to prepare children for a democratic world... we must build schools that are democratic. If we want responsible citizens, we must stop raising manageable ones.

Lenka Mazáková offers a personal counterpart to this systemic argument. She recalls the moment she stepped away from positional authority: "When I stopped standing behind the 'I know best' wall, something unexpected happened: I met the children as equals."

That shift, though risky, created space for real connection. She also challenged the idea that quality learning should happen in comfort:

Comfort seems to be a weak teacher. Real learning begins when something breaks down... Children grow when they face challenges and figure out what to do.

For Lenka, comfort is a weak teacher. Authentic learning begins when groups fail, when disagreements surface, when a train is missed and the plan breaks down. Growth comes through struggle, not avoidance. She now embraces what she calls "mandatory tasting," the chance for children to encounter ideas, values, and experiences they might never choose on their own. Unplanned sparks (e.g., a strange video, or a debate overheard on the bus) can shift perspectives more than carefully planned lessons. To her, learning freedom means balancing direction with openness, resisting the urge to over-script children's journeys.

REDEFINING THE ROLE OF THE ADULT

The team at the **Slobodná Škola** in Slovakia articulates this as a redefinition of the adult's role:

Our task is to hold the space where learning may happen—not to force it to happen... True consent means they choose because it matters to them, not because it pleases us.

This requires living with discomfort: choices that look boring or chaotic, slow progress, and parental fears about productivity. "Freedom sounds great on paper—but in practice, it's slow, unpredictable, hard to measure. People want safety. And the old system, despite all its flaws, promises clarity."

Yet they return to trust as a necessary condition in schools, because in discomfort there is honesty, and in honesty, trust. "We keep choosing discomfort... because in that space, we find honesty. And in honesty, we build trust."

Taken together, these voices echo across contexts: digital and ecological, political and personal, formal and informal. From Prague to Vietnam, from Mexico to Slovakia, their reflections converge on a basic principle: freedom in learning is fragile, but it is also resilient.

EMERGENT PATTERNS

Stepping back from the individual stories and contexts, it becomes clear that these reflections form a constellation of recurring prioritie. Among the respondents, there is a shared undercurrent in diverse experiences of breaking away from old practices toward redefining learning freedom.

Rejecting speed as a measure of success

One of the strongest points of convergence is the critique of speed as an indicator of quality. While rapid progress is often celebrated in institutional and political narratives, these contributors see it as a false economy. This suggests a trade-off that sacrifices depth, connection, and human well-being.

As one contributor noted, rushing can take many forms: compressing curricula into unrealistic timelines, demanding immediate results from new reforms, or expecting learners to perform at a uniform pace regardless of context. Others describe how political decision-making compounds the problem, prioritizing visible quick wins over sustained change. This "hurry up" culture narrows the scope for exploration, risk-taking, and meaningful reflection, threatening the very conditions where learning deepens.

In different ways, they remind us that the most transformative learning often unfolds at a pace that resists measurement: the time it takes to build trust, to recover from setbacks, to integrate new understanding into lived experience.

Dismantling false measures

A second shared theme is the rejection of reductive metrics. While grades and rankings remain entrenched in many systems, these voices highlight their distorting effects, turning learning into a performance for external judgment rather than an authentic engagement with ideas.

Several contributors point out that such measures do more than misrepresent learning; they actively shape behavior in ways that undermine it. When students understand that their value will be reduced to a mark, they learn to prioritize what is tested over what is meaningful. Educators, too, can be drawn into teaching to the metric rather than to the learner.

This pattern extends beyond academic grading to encompass the broader culture of audit and inspection. Respondents describe how constant measurement can crowd out innovation, discouraging educators from experimenting with new approaches that may not yield immediately "measurable" results. They do not call for the abolition of evaluation outright, but for new forms of accountability that honor complexity, context, and growth over time.

Integrating rather than fragmenting

Many of the contributors see integration as both a pedagogical principle and a survival skill for the 21st century. In their accounts, learning that remains siloed (i.e., detached from lived realities and from other fields of knowledge) is incomplete and brittle.

Several point to the way real-world challenges resist neat categorization. Environmental issues, for example, require an interplay of scientific understanding, civic engagement, ethical reasoning, and communication. The same holds for the digital sphere, where technical literacy must be matched by media awareness, social empathy, and cultural fluency.

This integrative stance also extends to the boundaries between school and community. Contributors envision learning ecosystems where formal institutions are porous, connected to local contexts, global networks, and the full range of learners' interests. In these environments, integration serves as the default approach to cultivating knowledge and skills, not an enrichment activity on the periphery.

Trusting learners and letting go of control

A recurring thread is the belief that learners of all ages are capable of steering their own growth when given the trust and conditions to do so. For some, this trust is built into the structures they work within, such as democratic or self-directed schools. For others, it is a deliberate personal practice in more traditional settings, requiring conscious restraint from over-directing the process.

Contributors acknowledge that letting go of control is rarely easy. Adults must accept choices that may not align with their own plans or aesthetics, and that they resist intervening simply to speed up progress or tidy the process. Trust in this sense is built from an active stance that involves careful listening, honest dialogue, and a willingness to share responsibility.

Several also point out that trust works both ways. For learners to embrace autonomy, they must be able to trust that the adults around them will support rather than punish experimentation, and that mistakes will be treated as part of the process rather than as failures to be avoided. Learners respond to that trust with greater ownership of their learning, a willingness to take risks, and deeper engagement in the process.

Confronting systemic barriers

While personal and local practices matter, these contributors are acutely aware of the structural forces that shape what is possible in their contexts. Bureaucratic procedures, legislative constraints, and deeply ingrained cultural narratives about "what school should be" all influence the scope for change.

In some accounts, these barriers are logistical: rigid timetables, inflexible curriculum frameworks, or underfunding for alternative approaches. In others, they are ideological: mistrust of non-traditional pathways, resistance to student-led initiatives, or the framing of education primarily as workforce preparation.

Several participants observe that even well-intentioned policies can become obstacles when implemented without flexibility or attention to local needs. This is particularly evident when reforms are driven by political agendas, which can result in abrupt shifts of direction, fragmented programs, and the erosion of initiatives before they have time to take root.

Locating spaces of thriving

Despite the pressures, every contributor identifies places, however small, where learning freedom is alive. These spaces are often modest in scale and informal in structure, but they carry disproportionate influence in shaping what is possible.

Some of these are physical places: community workshops, intergenerational programs, or mixed-age learning groups where mutual teaching is valued. Others are relational spaces: circles of practice where peers mentor one another, or networks that connect learners across distances through shared projects.

What unites these thriving spaces is their responsiveness. They adapt to learners' needs rather than forcing learners to adapt to them. They allow for the unpredictability of genuine inquiry, and they treat autonomy as a lived reality rather than a slogan. Importantly, these spaces often exist at the margins of formal systems, which makes them both precious and vulnerable.

Across these six patterns, a single thread connects the stories. Learning freedom appears when educators permit risk of venturing into the unkown and accept a degree of fragility. It shows up when a student chooses a direction without preapproval, when a class follows an unplanned question, and when a community project crosses disciplinary borders without asking permission from the timetable. These moments face constant pressure from administrative routines, political demands, and the habit of reducing value to numbers. Yet learning freedom persists. It survives because individuals decide to defend it, even in places designed to contain it.

Our task is to see them as part of the same shift, one that prizes agency over compliance, depth over speed, and shared purpose over narrow performance. Learning freedom embraces trust, curiosity, and space to act. And in the long run, those are the conditions that allow education to flourish.

To read the full, unedited responses from contributors across all regions and contexts, scan the QR code and explore the collection online.

22

In the absence of hope, we must build communities of trust

Education faces a crisis of purpose. In many places, learning is no longer nurtured. It is managed. Books are banned. Teachers are silenced. Histories are erased or rewritten. Students who disagree are detained and deported. These actions reflect a growing comfort with authoritarian control, where education functions less as a path to knowledge than as a mechanism for enforcing obedience.

At the same time, the world that schools promise to prepare young people for is breaking apart and rebuilding in plain sight. Climate instability accelerates. Forced migration reshapes neighborhoods and nations. Artificial intelligence reorganizes labor, identity, and power. Digital platforms fracture shared reality and reward outrage over truth. These forces define daily life, yet most educational institutions remain tied to structures built for another century.

The common response calls for reform. Policymakers demand new standards, new accountability systems, new technologies, and new leadership. Reform misses the point. The deeper problem lies in assumptions that have guided schooling for generations. Systems assume control produces learning, standardization produces fairness, ranking produces motivation, and schooling exists to supply labor (Biesta, 2010). These systems do not malfunction. They perform exactly as designed. Reform efforts polish the machinery and preserve its logic (Tyack & Cuban, 1995). That is the trap.

Manifesto 25 rejects the idea that education needs repair. It argues education needs a new purpose. The shift must move from control to trust, from compliance to agency, from credentialing to becoming, from institutional priorities to human dignity and shared responsibility. Learners who will sustain democratic life, confront ecological collapse, and navigate manipulation require environments that cultivate courage, care, and discernment. The challenge is moral, not technical.

The manifesto does not claim to prescribe solutions. It offers a *shared language* for people who rethink education in their own contexts. It creates a *framework* for understanding across differences so communities can design their own roadmaps toward the future. The document emerged from conversations across regions and cultures. Contributors sought guidance from the Global South before turning to the North. Educators, organizers, and learners shaped the text with lived experience. The release invited signatures, remixes, and translations from the start. Individuals and organizations appear as co-authors to affirm collective ownership and collective responsibility.

The manifesto supports communities in imagining and building their best possible futures. These futures will not look uniform. They will look relevant, dignified, and grounded in human needs. The text challenges the belief that minor adjustments can rescue outdated systems. It calls for reimagining education from the ground up. Table 3 contrasts two models that express opposing assumptions about learning, authority, and meaning. These contrasts expose a conscious decision. Education can organize around control or around liberation. The choice shapes classrooms, policies, and daily relationships.

Table 3. Control vs. liberatory learning frameworks.

CONTROL-ORIENTED SYSTEMS	LIBERATORY LEARNING FRAMEWORKS
Compliance as a goal	Curiosity as a starting point
Standardized content and outcomes	Contextual and relational learning
Learning as preparation for defined workforce roles	Learning as a process of becoming
Knowledge delivered from authority	Knowledge co-constructed with others
Assessment as ranking	Assessment as reflection and growth
Surveillance and monitoring	Trust and autonomy
Teachers and staff as managers	Teachers and staff as collaborators
Curriculum shaped by state or corporate interests	Curriculum shaped by each learner's and community's needs
Legitimacy confined to formal institutions	Legitimacy grounded in lived experiences

WHEN HOPE COLLAPSES

Hope alone does not produce change. Many people believe policy, leadership, or innovation will improve education. Yet, in many contexts, authorities no longer neglect education. They weaponize it, use it to restrict knowledge, remove critical thought, and enforce obedience (Apple, 2006).

The United States, for example, currently has a Secretary of Education who confuses artificial intelligence with steak sauce (Silberling, 2025). This may seem like simple incompetence, but it is not. It reflects indifference (if not outright contempt) for public education. Those in power no longer pretend to care. They seek a population trained to obey, not to think. The means do not matter to them, only the outcomes they can control.

In this context, hope is not enough. *Manifesto 25* reminds us that when hope collapses, we must act. Not through violence, but through vision. Not through compliance, but through care. We must resist systems that reduce learning to conformity and build new ones based on trust, relevance, and shared responsibility.

There is no single answer to what education should become. Any meaningful response must emerge from local conditions, relationships, and histories. Attempts to standardize learning across diverse contexts often erase the very differences that make communities resilient. What matters most is defining clarity of purpose. We must decide what we are fighting for and what we are willing to leave behind. This is not a "fight" with fists or sticks—*but with vision*. With solidarity. With activated imagination. With creative action. And with communities built from trust.

CONFRONTING FEAR

As long as education systems operate through fear and anxiety, they will resist collaboration, silence dissent, and block innovation. Fear undermines the very relationships that make learning possible.

We need a new theory of action that recognizes trust as a precondition for meaningful change. This means designing approaches to education that invite participation, rather than compliance. It means listening to students and families as contributors, not consumers. It also means building partnerships across sectors. Governments, educators, parents, and businesses must engage one another not through mandates, but through mutual responsibility.

As outlined in *Knowmad Society* (Moravec, 2013), learners and other members of society are valued for their ability to adapt, collaborate, and apply knowledge across unpredictable settings. In that context, trust is the precondition for innovation. People need the freedom to take intellectual risks without fear of punishment or shame. Without trust, creativity stagnates and learning narrows.

From *Manifesto 25*:

> ***We can and must build cultures of trust in our schools and communities.*** *As long as our education systems continue to be based on fear, anxiety, and distrust, challenges to all of the above will persist. If educators are to build a collective capacity to transform education, we need engaged communities, and we also need to engage with the communities we serve. This requires a new theory of action, centered on trust, where students, schools, governments, businesses, parents, and communities may engage in collaborative initiatives to co-create new education futures.*

Purposive transformation begins with trust as a basic element that must be practiced, renewed, and protected. This includes trust in students, in educators, and in communities. It also requires institutions to trust that people will act in the interest of collective well-being when they are given the opportunity and support to do so.

Communities of trust are not uniform. They vary across geography, culture, and institutional setting. In some cases, they take the form of democratic schools, where decisions are made collectively by students and staff. In others, they emerge in informal learning hubs, mutual aid networks, or grassroots education coöperatives. What binds them is a shared commitment to honoring learners as full participants in shaping their educational journeys.

This approach has practical implications. In trust-based settings, educators often shift their roles from deliverers of content to facilitators of process. Relationships are emphasized over efficiency. Time is treated as flexible, allowing for deeper inquiry and reflection. Conflict is addressed as a site for learning, rather than as a disruption to be suppressed.

Building such communities also requires institutions to take risks with uncommon boldness. Trust cannot flourish in environments dominated by performance metrics or compliance checklists that ultimately remove trust from the system. Schools must be willing to question their own assumptions, redistribute authority, and invite participation from those who are often excluded from decision-making, especially youth, families, and marginalized communities.

Any meaningful response must grow from specific conditions, relationships, and histories. Efforts to standardize learning across diverse contexts often erase the differences that allow communities to adapt and persist. The challenge is to gain clarity of purpose and to define who we want to become. We must decide what to protect, what to change, and what to leave behind as we build new cultures of trust in our schools and communities.

23
Break the rules that break us

In classrooms built for obedience, success often means staying inside the lines, even as the world outside demands we redraw them. Today's schools reward silent conformity over courageous inquiry, sending an implicit message to learners: don't ask too much, don't reach too far (hooks, 1994).

OBEDIENCE IS NOT LEARNING.

This compliance-first culture undermines our collective capacity to adapt, innovate, and think critically about the complexities facing our societies and planet. As the world around us grows increasingly unpredictable, a fundamental choice emerges: Will education continue to reinforce outdated structures, or will we empower students and educators to thoughtfully rewrite the rules?

Yet not all rules are oppressive, and not all disobedience is virtuous. Some rules protect safety, equity, and inclusion. So how do we distinguish meaningful resistance from chaos or self-interest?

Moving forward requires empowering learners and educators with the clarity to understand why rules exist and the courage to challenge them when they no longer serve the common good. This reflective disruption begins by openly questioning our assumptions: *Why do we learn the way we do? Whose interests do current systems serve? What might education look like if we built it intentionally for our young people and communities rather than obediently for the benefit of the "other?"*

From *Manifesto 25*:

> ***Break the rules, but understand why clearly first.*** *Our school systems are built on cultures of obedience, enforced compliance, and complacency. The creativity of students, staff, and our institutions is inherently stultified. It is easier to be told what to think than to think for ourselves. Openly asking questions and building a metacognitive awareness of what we have created and what we would like to do about it can best cure this institutionalized malaise. Only then can we engineer justified breaks from the system that challenge the status quo and have the potential to create real impact.*

To educate effectively for the future, we must distinguish clearly between blind obedience and thoughtful engagement. Learners may then begin to critically and creatively rewrite the rules of education itself.

CULTURES OF COMPLIANCE GOT US HERE

Today's school structures, rooted in industrial-era values of efficiency and control, continue to prioritize standardization over individuality. Surveillance technologies track student behavior, teachers navigate strict curricula with limited autonomy, and the true complexity of learning is often reduced to simple metrics like test scores and grades. Consequently, curiosity is treated as a distraction, creative thinking becomes risky, and genuine questioning is perceived as defiance.

When learners and educators internalize the idea that compliance is the safest route to success, obedience becomes a survival strategy. Over time, this mindset erodes both creativity and critical thought, transforming education into a passive experience rather than an active exploration of knowledge and possibility.

The implications of such compliance-driven education are profound. Students become passive recipients rather than empowered creators of knowledge. Teachers act as gatekeepers rather than facilitators of inquiry. In emphasizing rule-following, many schools unintentionally suppress the one thing the future demands most: imaginative response to uncertainty.

To transform this reality, we must first recognize the outdated logic at its core. Our educational structures were never designed to foster creativity or genuine innovation. Clearly understanding this historical context is essential before we can thoughtfully and intentionally rework schools into spaces that reflect today's social and civic realities.

MEANINGFUL ACTION REQUIRES CRITICAL THINKING

Not all acts of disruption create meaningful change. For any intervention to have lasting impact, it must emerge from a place of thoughtful understanding. Breaking rules without first knowing why they exist can lead to confusion rather than transformation (Biesta, 2013). To equip learners to effectively disrupt outdated systems, we must cultivate the critical skill of *metacognition*, or "thinking about thinking" (see esp. Mezirow, 1997).

Before disrupting systems, learners need tools to think critically and reflectively. Practices like student-led investigations, classroom dialogue, and participatory decision-making help develop the insight necessary for intentional action.Classrooms can foster critical consciousness through collaborative questioning, reflective dialogue, and student-driven investigations. For example, when students trace how grading policies affect motivation, or how class schedules shape wellbeing, abstract systems become tangible and reform becomes actionable.

Similarly, embedding democratic decision-making in classrooms and schools gives students real opportunities to practice collective responsibility (Kahne & Westheimer, 2003). When learners actively debate policies, propose reforms, and experience firsthand the complexities of consensus-building, they shift from abstract critique to practical, purposeful engagement. Together, metacognition and critical thinking build the bridge between awareness and action, offering learners the clarity to understand the rules, and the courage to imagine something better.

PURPOSIVE DISOBEDIENCE:
DESIGNING MEANINGFUL DISRUPTION

When students and educators develop a clear, critical understanding of their educational systems, they become ready to disrupt those systems purposefully. Purposive, purposive disobedience is intentional rule-breaking grounded in reflection, insight, and careful consideration. It differs sharply from defiance or chaos because it emerges from clarity about what needs changing and why.

Civil rights leader and U.S. Congressman John Lewis famously encouraged "good trouble," carefully considered acts of resistance against unjust systems. Applying this concept to education reveals powerful instances where students and educators have thoughtfully challenged the status quo to create meaningful improvements.

Consider the students who have challenged biased curricula, successfully advocating for more inclusive syllabi that highlight diverse perspectives and previously marginalized voices. In the United States and elsewhere, high school students have petitioned districts to include literature representing a broader spectrum of experiences, significantly enriching educational conversations.

Educators, too, have practiced purposive disobedience. Many teachers have shifted away from conventional grading to narrative feedback and portfolio assessments, focusing on genuine student growth rather than numerical scores (Wiliam, 2011; Darling-Hammond & Snyder, 2000). While initially met with resistance, these carefully considered changes have often fostered deeper engagement, intrinsic motivation, and trust within classrooms (Shepard, 2000; Reeve, 2012; Deci & Ryan, 1985).

Schools themselves can embody purposive disobedience. Innovation-oriented institutions such as High Tech High (United States) and Lumiar (Brazil) actively question traditional structures, replacing standardized curricula with student co-designed projects and community-based learning experiences. These schools demonstrate that thoughtfully challenging educational conventions can lead to greater creativity, innovation, and student agency.

These examples succeed precisely because their disruptions are grounded in careful reflection, not reaction. Purposive disobedience is ultimately an act of care, responsibility, and civic engagement, designed to create better outcomes for learners and communities alike. It recognizes that some rules no longer serve their original purpose, and that challenging those rules is necessary for meaningful educational evolution.

Far from simply defying authority, purposive disobedience embraces collective responsibility, using thoughtful disruption to build educational systems that are more humane, equitable, and responsive.

FROM INDIVIDUAL ACTS TO SYSTEMIC SHIFTS

Individual acts of purposive disobedience can ignite meaningful change, but isolated efforts rarely transform entrenched systems. For lasting impact, intentional disruptions must connect, amplify each other, and embed themselves into broader educational cultures.

Schools committed to genuine transformation must intentionally cultivate environments where critique and thoughtful questioning are celebrated rather than suppressed (Westheimer & Kahne, 2004). Open forums, student advisory councils, educator-led inquiry groups, and community dialogues create safe and structured spaces for meaningful conversation about what education should achieve and how existing rules support or hinder those goals.

Professional development must go beyond pedagogy and teach facilitation of disruption (Senge *et al.*, 2012). Beyond instructional techniques, educators need training in facilitating change processes, supporting student-led initiatives, and fostering metacognitive reflection. By becoming comfortable with uncertainty and skilled at guiding thoughtful disruption, teachers evolve into change leaders who inspire and sustain innovation.

Recognizing and rewarding innovation, even when it challenges established norms, is crucial. Public acknowledgment, inclusion of innovative practices in official school policies, and dedicated resources for experimentation signal that thoughtful questioning is valued. This cultural shift reinforces the idea that purposive disobedience is an exercise of responsible leadership toward improved outcomes.

Finally, educational change must align with broader social movements advocating democratic participation, social justice, and sustainability. Schools are mirrors of their communities; thus, purposive disobedience within education can significantly contribute to societal progress. When educational reform connects to wider movements for equity and sustainability, it gains deeper purpose and wider impact. This includes broadening the rebellion to teacher unions, student alliances, and policy influencers, each able to act in their capacities to bring about systemic shifts.

By fostering thoughtful, purposeful acts of disobedience, schools prepare learners to thoughtfully and actively shape a more equitable and just society.

NOW THAT WE KNOW *WHY*, GO AHEAD, BREAK THE RULES

Lasting transformation begins not with rebellion, but with reflection. Change-makers must know the rules well enough to rewrite them with clarity and purpose.

This process requires continuous dialogue: questioning whose interests current rules serve, exploring who benefits or suffers from compliance, and imagining more equitable, humane possibilities. Learners and educators must be provided agency to ask these critical questions and also to act decisively on their answers.

If we truly seek to educate for the future, we must nurture and embrace reflective disruptors who understand rules clearly enough to challenge and rewrite them purposefully. Thoughtful rebellion is an act of courage and imagination. It is an invitation to move beyond obedience and toward collective creativity.

Break the rules…but only after learning how they were built, and who they were built for. Then, build something braver. Something wilder. Something more just.were built for. Then, build something braver. Something wilder. Something more just.

24
Activism as learning: When students teach the system a lesson

What if we viewed activism not as learning's most authentic expression? Students learn more from raising their voices than raising their hands. When they organize protests, launch mutual aid projects, or speak truth to power, they step into their learning. Yet schools rarely acknowledge these moments as education. When students organize mutual aid networks or stage walkouts, adults often view them as distractions from learning, not demonstrations of it.

Too often, institutions treat activism as a threat to order rather than a form of civic literacy. This marginalization reflects risk aversion and a deeper discomfort with student power. When young people speak truth to systems, they expose contradictions between what schools claim to teach (e.g., critical thinking, democratic participation) and what they often demand: absolute compliance.

Activism creates conditions for what Freire (1970) called *conscientização* (awakening through reflection and action), a dialogic process of developing critical awareness through reflection and praxis. Where Freire critiques passive, 'banking' models of education, Dewey (1938) insists that all genuine learning must grow out of lived experience. Lave and Wenger (1998) take this further by framing learning as participation in communities of practice, where identity and knowledge co-evolve through engagement. Activism, in this light, becomes an example of experiential learning and a model of communal, justice-oriented inquiry.

Activism does not need to be thought of as a learning detour. Where Freire demands critical action, Dewey locates growth in real-world inquiry. Together, they frame activism not disruptively, but as the deepest mode of learning and its most urgent expression. And as Lave and Wenger's (1998) theory of communities of practice suggests, real learning takes root when people engage meaningfully with others around shared goals and challenges. Activism is such a community: relational, improvisational, and deeply situated.

From *Manifesto 25*:

> ***Activism is a space where unlearning thrives.*** *Whether through non-violent civil disobedience, street protests, artistic demonstrations, or performative resistance, activism challenges the status quo and rebuilds from the ground up. It teaches resilience, agency, and the courage to confront broken systems, including education itself. Educators must embrace activism as a core learning tool, transforming passive learners into active participants in shaping the world.*

We need to move beyond viewing activism as a supplementary arena for learning and recognize it as a pedagogical framework in its own right, blending praxis, reflection, and action with emotional and civic literacy.

Activism cultivates urgency, judgment, and emotional depth. These are capacities schools often struggle to nurture. It shifts the learner from spectator to participant, from absorbing content to shaping context. If we want young people to imagine better futures, we must let them challenge the systems that block the way.

Of course, activism as pedagogy is not without criticism. Not all student-led movements succeed. Power dynamics between youth and adults can constrain dialogue. And for marginalized students, civic participation may carry higher risks. Yet these challenges are reasons to integrate it thoughtfully, with attention to safety, reflection, and context.

THE LEARNING WORK OF ACTIVISM

Activism begins when young people choose to speak up, step in, or organize for something better. That decision marks a powerful act of agency, and the learning that follows flows directly from it.

By engaging in activism, students enter a discovery process they direct to confront injustice. They frame the questions that matter, challenge flawed assumptions, and experiment with strategies to navigate complexity. Activism becomes a civic apprenticeship where learners design and lead the change they seek.

This learning unfolds in real time and under real pressure. Organizing a walkout demands coördination, persuasive messaging, media literacy, and emotional risk-taking. Creating a public mural requires historical research, aesthetic judgment, and negotiation with stakeholders. Writing an open letter calls for strategic tone, ethical reasoning, and evidence-based advocacy. Occupying a school building to protest underfunding or unfair policy becomes an immersive lesson in law, power dynamics, endurance, and collective decision-making. Every step reinforces the sense that students' choices carry weight.

More importantly, students drive this learning themselves. No one assigns the protest. No rubric scores the coalition. They act out of conviction because the issues they confront are lived, local, and urgent, not hypothetical or distant.

Research on civic engagement and youth participatory action shows that this kind of self-directed activism builds lasting competencies as a form of action research (Cammarota & Fine, 2008). It strengthens agency, nurtures critical consciousness, and cultivates the persistence to stay engaged even when change feels slow or uncertain. These are the dispositions young people need to thrive in democracies, solve complex problems, and build more just futures.

Schools can't script this kind of growth, but they can nurture it. Educators can recognize activism as a valid form of learning, help students analyze their experiences, and link them to broader systems and ideas. They can shift the question from "What assignment did you complete?" to "What change did bring into the world?" When students organize, question, resist, and reimagine, they engage in some of the deepest learning available connected to their power to shape the world.

ACTIVISM AS A SOURCE OF RESILIENCE AND BELONGING

Through actions such as die-ins, mutual aid networks, and underground libraries, students demonstrate mastery of media strategy, coalition-building, and
radical care. These are capacities developed through embodied, improvisational
learning. They curate narratives, manage logistics, interpret law, collaborate
under stress, and speak with moral clarity under real-world stakes.

No quiz prepares students for these actions. No curriculum fully contains
them. Yet the learning runs deep. Students sharpen strategy, negotiate conflict,
and refine values through trial, iteration, and care. They become learners and
leaders in the same breath.

Of course, integrating activism into educational practice raises ethical
questions such as *how can educators support student-led change without impos-
ing ideology?* The answer lies in cultivating the habits of civic inquiry, systems
analysis, and reflection that undergird principled action. Supporting student
agency requires pedagogical courage. In this, educators have a role as guides.
They can ask: *What are you learning from this? What comes next? How does this
connect to others before you?*

Across the globe, students already lead. In Kerala, they blend ecological wisdom
with digital activism. In Santiago, they disrupt transit systems to protest
inequality. In Minneapolis, students and staff build unscripted curriculum from
community grief. This is real education.

When students act for change, they learn how to show up for others,
how to support their values, and how to build the futures they dare to imagine.
As Kirshner (2009) argues, youth-led activism provides a unique context for
developing civic identity, where young people understand the mechanics of
power and practice influencing it. By organizing campaigns, negotiating with
adults, and mobilizing peers, students gain practical experience with leadership,
collective decision-making, and strategic communication. These activities
cultivate a deeper sense of belonging and personal efficacy.

Students come to see themselves as learners within a system, and as
agents capable of shaping that system. The learning that emerges from activism
is both social and developmental: it nurtures solidarity, strengthens problem-

solving, and embeds young people in communities of practice where values are tested, adapted, and enacted in real time.

If we want students to build better futures, we must give them room to question the present and the power to change it. Activism completes the educational experience. *What if schools did not only tolerate youth activism, but also learned from it? What if education itself became an act of liberation?*

25
Question everything

In our era defined by radical uncertainty, a primary duty of education should be to develop our courage to question relentlessly. Otherwise, we will never learn. We must go beyond merely interrogating the facts presented to us or the authorities that deliver them. It demands that we scrutinize everything, especially including our most fundamental beliefs, the frameworks we rely on, and critically, our own roles within these constructs. Without such introspection, education risks becoming a tool of conformity rather than a catalyst for insight.

We find ourselves at a pivotal crossroads, caught between systemic collapse and unprecedented possibility. The rise of artificial intelligence challenges the very nature of knowledge itself, pushing us to reconsider what it means to be human, what capacities are uniquely ours, and how we define intelligence and creativity. Simultaneously, the accelerating pace of climate breakdown tears apart long-held certainties, exposing the inadequacy of traditional models and demanding adaptive thinking that transcends outdated paradigms.

Amid these upheavals, political landscapes across the globe are hardening into rigid authoritarian regimes, where conformity is enforced and dissent is met with repression. In such environments, education systems that reward obedience and suppress critical thinking become complicit in maintaining oppression. To educate in this context by fostering passive acceptance will lead to negative consequences, as it undermines the very agency necessary for individuals and societies to navigate and survive profound transformation.

The world is moving faster than education can adapt. We have no time for schooling systems disguised as achievement factories that churn out replicas of the status quo. Such systems prepare learners for a world that no longer exists and for problems they will never be asked to solve. Questioning cannot be treated as a classroom technique. It must become a civic habit and a personal discipline, practiced in how we learn, how we teach, and how we decide what is factual. This is how we claim agency.

From *Manifesto 25*:

> ***Question everything.** Start with this manifesto. Blind acceptance breeds complacency. As co-learners, we must provide safe spaces to critically evaluate all ideas, including the ones presented here. By contributing to a culture of critical thinking and open dialogue, the development of one's self-awareness is encouraged and individuals are enabled to contribute toward a continuous evolution of how we teach and learn.*

Mainstream educational institutions operate as engines of standardization. They applaud compliance and punish the boldness of disruption. Doubt becomes an enemy, difference a liability. Under the banner of consistency, we erase the beauty of individual uniqueness. In pursuit of uniform excellence, we flatten diversity. This pact to stop questioning is how systems preserve their power.

The act of questioning is never purely intellectual; it demands emotional bravery. To challenge our deepest beliefs, and to expose the fragile ground beneath our assumptions, is to face uncertainty in its rawest form. This is why the manifesto insists on safe spaces for critical evaluation: because true questioning unfolds within relationships of trust and vulnerability. The courage to question grows not only from reason but from feelings: doubt, discomfort, fear, and sometimes grief. Education must support this embodied process, recognizing that intellectual freedom is inseparable from emotional resilience and communal care. Self-awareness emerges when we learn to hold complexity in our hearts as well as our minds.

But education, fundamentally, should not be about maintaining the status quo; it should about enabling the creation of what could be. True creation, authentic transformation, is never frictionless. It requires tension, disagreement, and the courage to embrace uncertainty.

QUESTION TO LEARN, UNLEARN, AND RELEARN

We must tear down education's stifling walls and reconstruct it as a culture of bold inquiry. This demands making intentional room for discomfort, contradiction, and unresolved questions. We need learning environments brave enough to challenge conventional rules, dominant assumptions, and accepted truths. Together, students and educators must dismantle received wisdom, not merely to deconstruct but to reconstruct deeper, shared meanings.

To question is to embark on the demanding journey of unlearning (Mezirow, 1991). Education often reinforces assumptions, biases, and norms so deeply ingrained they become invisible. The manifesto challenges us to discard what no longer holds, but this discarding is neither swift nor easy. Unlearning requires deliberate effort, patience, and support to uproot internalized prejudices and outdated paradigms (Mezirow, 1991; Brookfield, 2017). It is a process of making space, clearing the mental and emotional clutter so that new, more expansive ways of knowing can emerge. This labor is vital for genuine critical inquiry and for the self-awareness that the manifesto celebrates. Without unlearning, questioning risks remaining superficial, trapped by the very structures it seeks to challenge.

Unlearning is a communal, iterative process. It requires collective support to dismantle ingrained biases and to resist the pull of comfortable narratives. Spaces of uncommon safety become critical arenas where individuals can confront internalized oppression and open pathways toward new, shared ways of knowing.

This endeavor is inherently political, profoundly uncomfortable, and essential. bell hooks (1994) reminds us that true education is liberation, an act of deliberate transgression. Paulo Freire (1970) taught us that learners must be empowered as active agents shaping their own knowledge, not passive recipients of someone else's agenda. To educate critically is to reject intellectual domination and to affirm every individual's right (and obligation) to interpret the world actively, critically, and collaboratively.

SO, CONCRETELY, WHAT DOES THIS VIBRANT CULTURE OF QUESTIONING LOOK LIKE?

Questioning breaks the mold of scripted learning. It erupts when people reclaim the power to redefine what and how they learn, moving away from being passive consumers toward co-creators of their own intellectual journeys. It demands educators shed the guise of certainty and instead stand alongside learners as fellow explorers, unafraid to expose doubts and wrestle with unknowns in full view.

This process is messy, raw, and unapologetic. It is highly political. It thrives where communities refuse silence around uncomfortable realities (i.e., race, power, history) not to settle for easy answers but to ignite honest reckoning and collective imagining. It fuels the capacity to see through manipulation, dismantle myths taught by institutions, and craft new understandings that challenge the status quo.

Questioning everything is a radical, often risky act. It unsettles power, disrupts comfort, and threatens entrenched interests. The manifesto's invitation to start by questioning itself is a profound gesture of humility, and an acknowledgment of the dangers inherent in intellectual openness. For learners and educators alike, the choice to question may mean facing resistance, exclusion, or worse. Recognizing this reality is not to deter inquiry but to call for resilience and solidarity. Safe spaces become not just places of comfort but zones of courageous defiance where questioning is sustained against social and political pressures. To educate critically, then, is to build communities that protect and empower those who dare to ask the hard questions.

Here, education is a living experiment in freedom, where minds break open and new possibilities take shape.

IN LIEU OF CONCLUSION ...

This culture of inquiry toward improvement must include our own works, including *Manifesto 25* itself. Question every claim presented here. Challenge its assumptions. Discard what proves inadequate. Remix ideas that resonate. Infuse it with your own lived experiences, fresh perspectives, and emerging insights. Start at the edges and then dive deep. Texts should never be treated as sacred or beyond reproach. They are snapshots, made with the best storytelling mechanisms available at the moment. Their true value lies in being contested, reshaped, and actively claimed by those eager to build a better world.

Questioning, after all, is fundamentally creative. It is an intellectual act, often politically charged, inevitably disruptive, and ultimately generative. Questioning prepares us for the unknown and enables us to step forward into new possibilities by disrupting narratives that protect power and creating spaces for new stories that reflect diverse experiences and the future. This narrative transformation is both an act of liberation and a foundation for imagining and building alternative possibilities.

By questioning, we assert collective ownership of our shared futures. Ownership carries responsibility to collaboratively imagine, construct, and transform our world as active architects of what lies ahead. Our futures are not for others to design. They are ours.

Start by asking fiercer, sharper questions. Then collaboratively create answers worthy of them. Our futures await.

LET'S BEGIN.

CAHIER FIVE

Communities building new futures

FRAMING

The closing principles of Manifesto 25 emphasize that education is not a finished design but a living provocation. The manifesto does not offer a blueprint. It invites readers and communities to take what resonates, discard what does not, and create their own commitments. This openness reflects a deeper truth: change in education is collective. It happens when communities organize, resist containment, and experiment with new ways of learning together.

Across the world, such movements already exist. Some are formal, such as networks of democratic schools or community universities. Others emerge informally, in grassroots learning circles, mutual aid networks, or digital collaborations. What they share is a refusal to accept education as something imposed from above. They treat education as survival and freedom, as a way of cultivating agency in the face of crisis.

These movements highlight the importance of community in shaping futures. Learning is rarely an individual act; it depends on relationships, shared resources, and collective imagination. Communities transmit knowledge, preserve traditions, and build new practices. They also hold institutions accountable when education strays from its purpose. When communities claim ownership of education, they redefine it as a common good rather than a service to be consumed.

This orientation is vital in an era marked by instability. Climate change, authoritarian politics, and technological disruption challenge the capacity of centralized systems to respond effectively. Communities often see problems first and feel their effects most directly. They are also positioned to generate context-specific solutions. When schools align with community struggles for justice, sustainability, and inclusion, they contribute to resilience rather than perpetuate vulnerability.

Making education one's own requires courage. It involves questioning long-standing practices, breaking with logics that serve power, and imagining alternatives. It asks teachers to step out of scripts, students to claim agency, and parents to demand relevance. It asks policymakers to listen to those most affected rather than to the most powerful. Such actions are rarely comfortable, but they are necessary if education is to regain trust and legitimacy.

The final invitation of *Manifesto 25* is to act: to defend what matters, to retire what no longer serves, and to build what is missing. Each person and community will answer differently. For some, it may mean establishing a student-led council with real decision-making power. For others, it may involve embedding sustainability into every aspect of school life. For others still, it may mean rejecting standardized tests and adopting authentic forms of assessment. The point is not conformity but creativity.

Education becomes powerful when it is reclaimed as a practice of freedom. This does not mean freedom from responsibility but freedom (and responsibility) to act with purpose. Communities that take ownership of education demonstrate that futures can be shaped, not merely awaited. The work is never finished, but it is always possible.

This fifth cahier invites you to consider what it means to make education your own. It asks you to reflect on what you want to defend, what you are ready to let go of, and what you are prepared to create. These are not abstract questions. They are choices that shape lives, communities, and generations.

PROMPTS FOR REFLECTION

1. **Resonance and refusal.** Which principles of *Manifesto 25* do you most want to defend? Which do you reject or feel compelled to rewrite? Why?
2. **Making the manifesto your own.** If you were to write your own three-point manifesto for education, what would it say? Who would it serve, and who would it challenge?
3. **Struggle and change.** What does "fighting for change" look like in your context (practically, ethically, and collectively)? What risks are you willing to take, and what lines are you unwilling to cross?
4. **Community as power.** Where have you seen communities shape education from below? What lessons can you take from them for your own classroom, school, or neighborhood?
5. **Defend / discard / create.** What practices in your learning environment must be defended at all costs? What should be abandoned now? What is missing that you are ready to build?

Try this

Draft a mini-manifesto (3–5 points) for your classroom, school, or community. Share it with at least one group or partner. Revise it together, and let it guide one real decision within the coming weeks.

Notes

Now
Write your own manifesto

MY MANIFESTO

MY MANIFESTO

MY MANIFESTO♡

MY MANIFESTO♡

MY MANIFESTO♡

MY MANIFEST♡

MY MANIFESTO

MY MANIFESTO

MY MANIFESTO ♡

MY MANIFESTO ♡

MY MANIFESTO

LET'S CONTINUE

The journey of building a positive rebellion does not end here. Scan the QR code to access an online companion with resources aligned to each chapter. This collection evolves over time, adding research, cases, and practical tools so you can continue learning, teaching, and experimenting beyond what fits in print.

References and further reading

1EdTech. (n.d.). *Open badges.* https://openbadges.org

Anderson, J., & Winthrop, R. (2025). *The disengaged teen: Helping kids learn better, feel better, and live better.* Penguin Random House.

Apple, M. W. (2004). *Ideology and curriculum* (3rd ed.). Routledge.

Apple, M. W. (2006). *Educating the right way: Markets, standards, God, and inequality.* Routledge.

Au, W. (2009). *Unequal by design: High-stakes testing and the standardization of inequality.* Routledge.

Ball, S. J. (2003). The teacher's soul and the terrors of performativity. *Journal of Education Policy, 18*(2), 215–228. https://doi.org/10.1080/0268093022000043065

Bandura, A. (1997). *Self-efficacy: The exercise of control.* W. H. Freeman.

Barron, B. (2006). Interest and self-sustained learning. *Human Development, 49*(4), 193–224.

Biesta, G. (2010). *Good education in an age of measurement.* Paradigm.

Biesta, G. (2013). *The beautiful risk of education.* Routledge.

Bransford, J. D., Brown, A. L., & Cocking, R. R. (Eds.). (2000). *How people learn: Brain, mind, experience, and school.* National Academies Press.

Brookfield, S. D. (2017). *Becoming a critically reflective teacher* (2nd ed.). Jossey-Bass.

Brown, B. (2021). *Atlas of the heart: Mapping meaningful connection and the language of human experience.* Random House.

Brown, J., & Duguid, P. (2000). *The social life of information.* Harvard Business School Press.

Brynjolfsson, E., & McAfee, A. (2014). *The second machine age.* Norton.

Cammarota, J., & Fine, M. (2008). *Revolutionizing education: Youth participatory action research in motion.* Routledge.

Carlin, G. (2005). *Life is worth losing.* https://georgecarlin.com/shop/life-worth-losing/

Chief, D. (2017). *The present and future of land-based education in Treaty #3.* University of Victoria. https://journals.uvic.ca/index.php/winhec/article/view/18565/7901

Cobo, C., & Moravec, J. W. (2011). *Aprendizaje invisible: Hacia una nueva ecología de la educación* [Invisible learning: Toward a new ecology of education]. Publicacions i Edicions de la Universitat de Barcelona.

Cochran-Smith, M., & Lytle, S. L. (2009). *Inquiry as stance: Practitioner research for the next generation.* Teachers College Press.

Cognitive bias codex. (n.d.). *Cognitive bias codex* [Graphic]. https://upload.wikimedia.org/wikipedia/commons/6/65/Cognitive_bias_codex_en.svg

Cuban, L. (2018). The flight of a butterfly or the path of a bullet? *American Journal of Education, 124*(2), 195–218.

Davenport, T. H. (1998). *Working knowledge: How organizations manage what they know.* Harvard Business School Press.

Darling-Hammond, L. (2004). From "separate but equal" to "No Child Left Behind": The collision of new standards and old inequalities. In D. Meier (Ed.), *Many children left behind: How the No Child Left Behind Act is damaging our children and our schools* (pp. 3–32). Beacon Press.

Darling-Hammond, L. (2010). *The flat world and education.* Teachers College Press.

Darling-Hammond, L., & Cook-Harvey, C. M. (2018). *Educating the whole child: Improving school climate to support student success.* Learning Policy Institute. https://learningpolicyinstitute.org/product/educating-whole-child-brief

Darling-Hammond, S., Fronius, T., Sutherland, H., Guckenburg, S., Petrosino, A., & Hurley, N. (2020). *Restorative justice in U.S. schools: An updated research review.* WestEd.

Darling-Hammond, L., & Snyder, J. (2000). Authentic assessment of teaching in context. *Teaching and Teacher Education, 16*(5–6), 523–545.

Deci, E. L., & Ryan, R. M. (1985). *Intrinsic motivation and self-determination in human behavior.* Plenum Press.

DeLapp, P. R. (2008). *Curriculum policy, controversy, and change: Minnesota's profile of learning, 1993 to 2003* (Doctoral dissertation). University of Minnesota. https://hdl.handle.net/11299/47727

Deleuze, G., & Guattari, F. (1987). Introduction: Rhizome. In *A thousand plateaus: Capitalism and schizophrenia* (Vol. 2, pp. 3–25). University of Minnesota Press.

Dewey, J. (1938). *Experience and education.* Macmillan.

Digital Promise. (2024, August 14). *A new approach to digital equity: A framework for states and schools.* https://digitalpromise.org/2024/08/14/a-new-approach-to-digital-equity-a-framework-for-states-and-schools/

Dijk, J. van (2020). *The digital divide.* Polity.

Downes, S. (2012). *Connectivism and connective knowledge: Essays on meaning and learning networks.* National Research Council Canada.

Downes, S. (2022). Connectivism. *Asian Journal of Distance Education, 17*(1). https://asianjde.com/ojs/index.php/AsianJDE/article/view/623

Drucker, P. F. (1993). The rise of the knowledge society. *The Wilson Quarterly, 17*(2), 52–72.

Durlak, J., Weissberg, R., Dymnicki, A., Taylor, R., & Schellinger, K. (2011). The impact of enhancing students' social and emotional learning. *Child Development, 82*(1), 405–432.

Dweck, C. S. (2006). *Mindset: The new psychology of success.* Random House.

Ertmer, P. A., & Ottenbreit-Leftwich, A. T. (2010). Teacher technology change: How knowledge, confidence, beliefs, and culture intersect. *Journal of Research on Technology in Education, 42*(3), 255–284.

EUDEC. (2023). *EUDEC guidance document.* https://eudec.org/about-us/guidance-document/

Falk, J. H., & Dierking, L. D. (2018). *Learning from museums* (2nd ed.). Rowman & Littlefield.

Fielding, M., & Moss, P. (2011). *Radical education and the common school.* Routledge.

Freire, P. (1970). *Pedagogy of the oppressed.* Herder and Herder.

Freire, P. (1994). *Pedagogy of hope: Reliving Pedagogy of the Oppressed* (R. R. Barr, Trans.). Continuum. (Original work published 1992)

Fromm, E. (1992). *The art of being.* Continuum.

Fullan, M. (2018). *Nuance: Why some leaders succeed.* Corwin.

Fullan, M., & Hargreaves, A. (2012). *Professional capital: Transforming teaching in every school.* Teachers College Press.

Fullan, M., Quinn, J., & McEachen, J. (2018). *Deep learning: Engage the world, change the world.* Corwin.

Gay, G. (2018). *Culturally responsive teaching* (3rd ed.). Teachers College Press.

Gladstone, B. (Producer). (1998, November 30). The science in science fiction [Radio broadcast episode]. In *Talk of the Nation*. National Public Radio. https://www.npr.org/2018/10/22/1067220/the-science-in-science-fiction

Gray, P. (2013). *Free to learn: Why unleashing the instinct to play will make our children happier, more self-reliant, and better students for life*. Basic Books.

Gray, P. (2023). *Self-directed education: Unschooling and democratic schooling*. Oxford University Press. https://doi.org/10.1093/acrefore/9780190264093.013.80

Greenberg, D. (1992). *Free at last: The Sudbury Valley School*. Sudbury Valley School Press.

Gregory, A., Clawson, K., Davis, A., & Gerewitz, J. (2016). The promise of restorative practices. *Journal of Educational and Psychological Consultation, 26*(4), 325–353.

Gregory, A., & Evans, K. R. (2020). *The starts and stumbles of restorative justice in education: Where do we go from here?* National Education Policy Center.

Guan, H., Horan, J., & Zhang, A. (2025, January 27). *Guardians of forensic evidence: Evaluating analytic systems against AI-generated deepfakes*. National Institute of Standards and Technology. https://doi.org/10.6028/NIST.PUB.959128

Harris, D. (2016). Rhizomatic education and Deleuzian theory. *Open Learning: The Journal of Open, Distance and e-Learning, 31*(3), 219–232.

Hartkamp-Bakker, C., & Martens, R. (2024). True choice and taking ownership of life: A qualitative study into self-determination in Sudbury model schools. *On the Horizon, 32*(2/3), 130–144. https://doi.org/10.1108/OTH-03-2024-0008

Holt, J. (1967). *How children learn*. Pitman.

Holt, J. (1970). *Freedom and beyond*. E. P. Dutton.

Hooks, b. (1994). *Teaching to transgress: Education as the practice of freedom*. Routledge.

HolonIQ. (n.d.). *Global learning landscape*. https://www.holoniq.com/global-learning-landscape

Hmelo-Silver, C. E. (2004). Problem-based learning: What and how do students learn? *Educational Psychology Review, 16*(3), 235–266.

Hursh, D. W. (2007). Assessing No Child Left Behind and the rise of neoliberal education reform. *American Educational Research Journal, 44*(3), 493–518.

Illich, I. (1971). *Deschooling society*. Harper & Row.

IPCC. (2023). *Climate change 2023: Synthesis report. Summary for policymakers*. Intergovernmental Panel on Climate Change. https://www.ipcc.ch/report/ar6/syr/

Ito, M., Gutiérrez, K., Livingstone, S., Penuel, B., Rhodes, J., Salen, K., … & Watkins, S. C. (2013). *Connected learning: An agenda for research and design*. Digital Media and Learning Research Hub.

Johansen, B. (2020). *Full-spectrum thinking: How to escape boxes in a post-categorical future*. Berrett-Koehler Publishers.

Jones, S., Barnes, S., Bailey, R., & Doolittle, E. (2017). Promoting social and emotional competencies in elementary school. *Future of Children, 27*(1), 49–72.

Kahne, J., & Westheimer, J. (2003). Teaching democracy: What schools need to do. *Phi Delta Kappan, 84*(9), 34–40. https://doi.org/10.1177/003172170308500109

Kaplan, M. S. (2002). Intergenerational programs in schools: Considerations of form and function. *International Review of Education, 48*(5), 305–334. https://doi.org/10.1023/A:1021231713392

Kapur, M. (2016). Examining productive failure, productive success, unproductive failure, and unproductive success in learning. *Educational Psychologist, 51*(2), 289–299.

Kirshner, B. (2009). Power in numbers: Youth organizing as a context for exploring civic identity. *Journal of Research on Adolescence, 19*(3), 414–440. https://doi.org/10.1111/j.1532-7795.2009.00601.x

Kirschner, P. A., & De Bruyckere, P. (2017). The myths of the digital native and the multitasker. *Teaching and Teacher Education, 67*, 135–142. https://doi.org/10.1016/j.tate.2017.06.001

Klein, J. (2015). *Interdisciplining digital humanities: Boundary work in an emerging field.* University of Michigan Press.

Kohn, A. (2000). *The case against standardized testing: Raising the scores, ruining the schools.* Heinemann.

Koretz, D. (2017). *The testing charade.* University of Chicago Press.

Lave, J., & Wenger, E. (1998). *Communities of practice: Learning, meaning, and identity.* Cambridge University Press.

Leask, B. (2015). *Internationalizing the curriculum.* Routledge.

Linn, R. L. (2000). Assessments and accountability. *Educational Researcher, 29*(2), 4–16.

Luckin, R. (2018). *Machine learning and human intelligence.* UCL Press.

Lumina Foundation. (2022). *Solutions to build a 21st century connected credentialing system.* https://www.luminafoundation.org/resource/solutions-to-build-a-21st-century-connected-credentialing-system/

McIntyre, L. (2018). *Post-truth.* MIT Press.

Meadows, D. (2008). *Thinking in systems.* Chelsea Green.

Meier, D. (1995). *The power of their ideas: Lessons for America from a small school in Harlem.* Beacon Press.

Merton, R. K. (1938). Social structure and anomie. *American Sociological Review, 3*(5), 672–682. https://doi.org/10.2307/2084686

Mezirow, J. (1991). *Transformative dimensions of adult learning.* Jossey-Bass.

Mezirow, J. (1997). Transformative learning: Theory to practice. *New Directions for Adult and Continuing Education, 1997*(74), 5–12. https://doi.org/10.1002/ace.7401

Miller, R. (2015). Learning, the future, and complexity: An essay on the emergence of futures literacy. *European Journal of Education, 50*(4), 513–523. https://doi.org/10.1111/ejed.12157

Miller, R. (2018). *Transforming the future: Anticipation in the 21st century.* UNESCO.

Miller, R., Latham, B., & Cahill, B. (2016). *Humanizing the education machine: How to create schools that turn disengaged kids into inspired learners.* Wiley.

Mitra, D. (2018). Student voice in secondary schools. *Journal of Educational Administration, 56*(5), 473-487. https://dx.doi.org/10.1108/JEA-01-2018-0007

Moravec, J. W. (Ed.). (2013). *Knowmad Society.* Education Futures. https://educationfutures.com/publications/knowmad-society/

National Research Council. (1998). *High stakes: Testing for tracking, promotion, and graduation.* National Academies Press.

Neha, T., Reese, E., Schaughency, E., & Taumoepeau, M. (2020). The role of whānau (New Zealand Māori families) for Māori children's early learning. *Developmental Psychology, 56*(8), 1518–1531. https://doi.org/10.1037/dev0000835

Newman, S., & Hutton-Yeo, A. (2008). Intergenerational learning and the contributions of older people. *Ageing Horizons, 8*, 31–39.

Nietzsche, F. (1996). *Human, all too human: A book for free spirits* (R. J. Hollingdale, Trans.). Cambridge University Press. (Original work published 1878)

Nonaka, I., & Takeuchi, H. (1995). *The knowledge-creating company: How Japanese companies create the dynamics of innovation.* Oxford University Press.

Nouri, A., Tokuhama-Espinosa, T. N., & Borja, C. (2022). *Crossing mind, brain, and education boundaries.* Springer.

Nussbaum, M. (2011). *Creating capabilities.* Harvard University Press.

OECD. (2016). *Teacher professionalism. Teaching in Focus* (No. 14). OECD Publishing. https://doi.org/10.1787/5jm3xgskpc40-en

OECD. (2018). *The future of education and skills: Education 2030—The OECD learning compass 2030.* Organisation for Economic Co-operation and Development. https://www.oecd.org/education/2030-project/

OECD. (2020). *The future of education and skills: Education and skills 2030 (Final report).* OECD Publishing. https://www.oecd.org/education/2030-project/

OECD. (2021). *OECD skills outlook 2021: Learning for life.* OECD Publishing. https://www.oecd.org/en/publications/oecd-skills-outlook-2021_0ae365b4-en.html

Pantić, N., & Florian, L. (2015). Developing teachers as agents of inclusion and social justice. *Education Inquiry, 6*(3). https://doi.org/10.3402/edui.v6.27311

Perkins, D. N. (1986). *Knowledge as design.* Lawrence Erlbaum Associates.

Polanyi, M. (1958). *Personal knowledge: Towards a post-critical philosophy.* University of Chicago Press.

Ravitch, D. (2010). *The death and life of the great American school system: How testing and choice are undermining education.* Basic Books.

Reeve, J. (2012). A self-determination theory perspective on student engagement. *Educational Psychologist, 47*(2), 88–107.

Reich, R. B. (2020). *The system: Who rigged it, how we fix it.* Alfred A. Knopf.

Robinson, K. (2011). *Out of our minds.* Capstone.

Rogoff, B. (2003). *The cultural nature of human development.* Oxford University Press.

Sahlberg, P. (2015). *Finnish lessons 2.0: What can the world learn from educational change in Finland?* Teachers College Press.

Sawyer, R. K. (2012). *Explaining creativity.* Oxford University Press.

Scardamalia, M., & Bereiter, C. (2010). A brief history of knowledge building. *Canadian Journal of Learning and Technology, 36*(1). https://doi.org/10.21432/T2QW2P

Selwyn, N. (2021). *Education and technology: Key issues and debates.* Bloomsbury.

Senge, P. (2006). *The fifth discipline.* Doubleday.

Senge, P. M., Cambron-McCabe, N., Lucas, T., Smith, B., & Dutton, J. (2012). *Schools that learn: A fifth discipline fieldbook for educators, parents, and everyone who cares about education* (Rev. ed.). Crown.

Shepard, L. A. (2000). The role of assessment in a learning culture. *Educational Researcher, 29*(7), 4–14.

Shute, V., & Becker, B. (2010). *Innovative assessment for the 21st century.* Springer.

Siemens, G. (2005). Connectivism: A learning theory for the digital age. *International Journal of Instructional Technology and Distance Learning, 2*(1), 3–10.

Siemens, G. (2007a). *The network is the learning* [Video]. YouTube. http://www.youtube.com/watch?v=rpbkdeyFxZw

Siemens, G. (2007b). Connectivism: Creating a learning ecology in distributed environments. *Didactics of microlearning. Concepts, discourses and examples,* 53-68. Waxmann.

Silaghi, D. L., & Popescu, D. E. (2025). A systematic review of blockchain-based initiatives in comparison to best practices used in higher education institutions. *Computers, 14*(4), 141. https://doi.org/10.3390/computers14040141

Silberling, A. (2025, April 10). The US Secretary of Education referred to AI as "A1," like the steak sauce. *TechCrunch.* https://techcrunch.com/2025/04/10/the-us-secretary-of-education-referred-to-ai-as-a1-like-the-steak-sauce/

Stucki, P. (2010). *Māori pedagogy, pedagogical beliefs and practices in a Māori Tertiary Institution.* (Doctoral dissertation). Massey University.

Sustainable Development Solutions Network. (n.d.). *SDG 4: Quality education*. https://dashboards.sdgindex.org/map/goals/SDG4

Teacher Task Force. (n.d.). *Teacher Task Force*. https://teachertaskforce.org

Thomas, D., & Brown, J. S. (2011). *A new culture of learning: Cultivating the imagination for a world of constant change*. CreateSpace Independent Publishing Platform.

Tondeur, J., van Braak, J., Ertmer, P. A., & Ottenbreit-Leftwich, A. (2012). Preparing pre-service teachers to integrate technology in education: A synthesis of qualitative evidence. *Computers & Education, 59*(1), 134–144.

Tyack, D., & Cuban, L. (1995). *Tinkering toward utopia: A century of public school reform*. Harvard University Press.

UNESCO. (2019). *Embracing a culture of futures thinking*. United Nations Educational, Scientific and Cultural Organization. https://unesdoc.unesco.org/ark:/48223/pf0000374112

UNESCO. (2021). *Reimagining our futures together: A new social contract for education*. United Nations Educational, Scientific and Cultural Organization. https://doi.org/10.54675/ASRB4722

UNESCO. (2025, October 27). *Deepfakes and the crisis of knowing*. UNESCO. https://www.unesco.org/en/articles/deepfakes-and-crisis-knowing

Valenzuela, A. (1999). *Subtractive schooling: US-Mexican youth and the politics of caring*. State University of New York Press.

Vinge, V. (1993). The coming technological singularity: How to survive in the post-human era. *Whole Earth Review*. https://edoras.sdsu.edu/~vinge/misc/singularity.html

Vosoughi, S., Roy, D., & Aral, S. (2018). The spread of true and false news online. *Science, 359*(6380), 1146–1151.

Wang, P. C., Huang, J. W., & Lee, D. C. (2023). Participation in intergenerational food and agriculture education programs effectively promotes place attachment. *International Journal of Environmental Research and Public Health, 20*(5), 4616. https://doi.org/10.3390/ijerph20054616

Watters, A. (2021). *Teaching machines: The history of personalized learning*. MIT Press.

Wenger, E. (1998). *Communities of practice*. Cambridge University Press.

Wenger-Trayner, E., & Wenger-Trayner, B. (2020). *Learning to make a difference: Value creation in social learning spaces*. Cambridge University Press.

Westheimer, J., & Kahne, J. (2004). What kind of citizen? The politics of educating for democracy. *American Educational Research Journal, 41*(2), 237–269. https://doi.org/10.3102/00028312041002237

Wiliam, D. (2011). *Embedded formative assessment*. Solution Tree Press.

World Bank. (2025, February 5). *EVOKE: Transforming education to empower youth*. https://www.worldbank.org/en/topic/edutech/brief/evoke-an-online-alternate-reality-game-supporting-social-innovation-among-young-people-around-the-world

World Economic Forum. (n.d.). *Strategic intelligence: Discover*. https://intelligence.weforum.org/discover

World Economic Forum. (2024). *The global risks report 2024*. World Economic Forum.

World Economic Forum. (2025). *The future of jobs report 2025*. World Economic Forum. https://reports.weforum.org/docs/WEF_Future_of_Jobs_Report_2025.pdf

Zehr, H. (2015). *The little book of restorative justice*. Skyhorse.

Zhao, Y. (2009). *Catching up or leading the way: American education in the age of globalization*. ASCD.

Zhao, Y. (2012). *World class learners*. Corwin.

Zhao, Y. (2018). *What works may hurt: Side effects in education*. Teachers College Press.

Colophon

**BUILD A POSITIVE REBELLION:
CREATE NEW EDUCATION FUTURES**
By John W. Moravec

Book design
Martine Eyzenga
diezijnvaardig.nl

Publisher
Education Futures LLC, Minneapolis, Minnesota
educationfutures.com

How to cite this book
Moravec, J. W. (2026). Build a positive rebellion:
Create new education futures. Education Futures.

ISBN (print edition): 979-8-9948831-0-5

Statement on the use of AI
Generative AI (ChatGPT-5.2) supported the final
copyediting process by aligning the manuscript
with Education Futures' style guide and publication
standards, and by assisting in conceptual stress
testing; the author reviewed all outputs and retains
full responsibility for the final text.

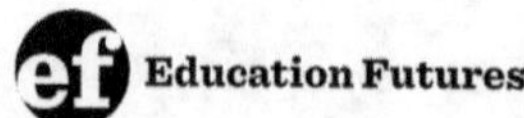